THE WRITER'S BOOK OF MEMORY

An Interdisciplinary Study for Writing Teachers

THE WRITER'S BOOK OF MEMORY

An Interdisciplinary Study for Writing Teachers

Janine Rider
Mesa State College

LAWRENCE ERLBAUM ASSOCIATES, PUBLISHERS
1995 Mahwah, New Jersey

Lawrence Erlbaum Associates, Inc., Publishers
10 Industrial Avenue
Mahwah, New Jersey 07430

Cover design by Susan Moore

Library of Congress Cataloging-in-Publication Data

The writer's book of memory : an interdisciplinary study for
writing teachers / by Janine Rider.
      p. cm.
     Includes bibliographical references and index.
     ISBN 0-8058-1980-0 (alk paper). -- ISBN 0-8058-
1981-9 (pbk. : alk. paper)
     1. English language--Rhetoric--Study and teaching.
     2. Autobiography--Authorship--Study and teaching.
     3. Memory.
     I. Title.
PE1404.R515 1995
808'.04207--dc20   95-18500
                                           CIP

Printed in the United States of America
10 9 8 7 6 5 4 3 2 1

This book is for *Kirk*
and for *Warren, Kent,* and *Hannah*

Contents

Preface

I was told some years ago that the rhetorical canon of memory had great potential for contemporary study but that no one was paying any attention to it. I was intrigued, and decided immediately that I would explore further. I discovered that the statement had been about 75% correct: Memory is a fascinating and relevant study, and the field is still largely unexplored; however, a number of excellent scholars have begun to consider memory's importance in contemporary rhetoric. Memory's time has arrived. A revival of interest in the canon of memory is especially important in a time when our memories are being influenced by huge technological changes in our culture—electronic databases or the well-wrought, 30-second Super Bowl commercial.

Philosophers and researchers alike ponder theories of knowledge-making, poets consider the sources of inspiration, and writing teachers foster prewriting. All of these activities are memorial: The memory is at work creating the product of our thoughts. I delighted in discovering how many scholars in different disciplines, places, and times have taken the powers of the memory seriously. My only problem was putting it all together. There is simply too much. So, although this book covers many disciplines and a great span of time, it is still not comprehensive. But it does set out to integrate a great deal of information and to show that in all fields of humanistic thought and in all efforts to write, memory is key. Without the retentive and, equally important, the reconstructive powers of memory, we know little and have nothing to say.

The general study of memory across the disciplines is interesting in itself. The focus of this volume, however, is on memory as a rhetorical canon, as a component of writing. It is crucial for those of us who write and teach writing to understand how completely memory governs the processes we undertake as we compose.

Memory is capricious, inventive, and untrustworthy, much like a clever but disobedient child. Yet on memory we construct our understanding of the world. I have used the "musings" that occur at the beginning of each chapter to illustrate how memory works—how my memory has embroidered the fabric of my reality.

Acknowledgments

When a working mother of three pursues a scholarly goal on top of everything else, many people make the effort possible. My ultimate critic, editor, and cheerleader is my husband Kirk, whose patience allowed me to write a book in my "spare" time and whose unerring command of language improved this work so much. My children—Warren, Kent, and Hannah—sacrificed all sorts of motherly treatment for the book. My special thanks go to Esther Broughton, my wonderful friend and colleague, who read my drafts over and over and gave so much generous encouragement.

I am grateful to my colleagues Sally Matchett, John Zeigel, and Myra Heinrich, who helped clarify my thinking in philosophy, literary criticism, and psychology. I owe much to my enthusiastic supporter Mark Hurlbert, who first suggested that memory might be worth writing about; to Joe Plummer, who talked me through the early stages of my ideas; and to Fred Reynolds, who encouraged me to complete my work on this book. Finally, I thank Jane VanDerWerff, the Mesa State College librarian who makes interlibrary loan work like overnight mail.

—*Janine Rider*

Chapter 1

Memory, Our Muse

Musings

I sat with a pen in one hand and a cup of coffee in the other, listening to my friend Joe Plummer talk about memory.

"Remember Proust? It was a petite madeleine and lime petal tea; he took a bite, drank a sip, and remembered everything about his past life: his aunt, her house, the town, the people ... and he wrote about it for 40 pages, all because of that cookie and tea."

"And Ingmar Bergman had an experience like that, too. He was walking along and saw a girl ride by on a bike. She had a yellow ribbon in her hair. The ribbon rustled in the breeze, brought up a memory, and suddenly the whole plot of Wild Strawberries came to Bergman in a flash."

"And do you remember the beginning of Portrait of the Artist? He's in the crib. He's supposedly remembering his life when he was just a baby."

Then Joe talked about Truman Capote, who memorized real, word-for-word conversations and used them in his book In Cold Blood. He improved his ability to remember by memorizing the encyclopedia, starting with a sentence a day, doing a bit more each day.

In Latin, memoria means "the thing remembered." Memoria is like a monument, Joe said; it's all we have. He was musing, and his mind was perking. We began to talk about the word musing: after all, Mnemosyne, or Memory, was the mother of the muses. Perhaps we are invoking memory when we invoke the muse. Is our creativity ever free from the past? No, we decided; nothing is ever free from the past. We talked about how often we had each wished that the muse was more available, and we laughed about the idea of invoking the muse with a phone call—1-800-245-MUSE.

For this study, that conversation was my first visit with the muse. The fact that memory had been forgotten as a useful canon of rhetoric was already obvious, and I had been thinking and reading about memory, but so far I had been without inspiration. Joe's morning musing began a search for information that led to my commitment to the idea that memory is a spring from which rhetoric flows.

I haven't tried to verify the things Joe told me that Saturday, and I'm not going to. Perhaps they're not quite accurate—maybe he remembered them wrong. Or maybe I am remembering incorrectly what he told me. Proust himself might not have been accurate, and Bergman might have later laughed at what someone recorded about him. One can't be sure. In fact, I thought Joe had told me that Capote practiced by memorizing the phone book; I was surprised when my notes said that it was the encyclopedia. But it doesn't matter. The point is that the information served me as a muse; it compelled me to add to my memory and it started the thought processes that led to this study, that made me want to invent a theory of memory. Memory is not a reliable, photographic image of the past. It is more than mere memorization, and we need to realize that. It is probably richer, just as a good piece of art is often richer than a photograph. However we look at memory, we must remember—it is all we have to help us understand our present and our future.

* * *

For most of my years as a writing teacher, I understood memory's place in rhetoric very narrowly. My understanding, shared with most of my colleagues and verified by writing textbooks, was that memory is a rhetorical canon irrelevant to writing. Classical rhetoric was divided into five parts or canons. As one of the five original canons of rhetoric, memory was fourth in the orator's speech-making process. First came invention, described as the consideration of all the possible arguments and approaches for making a case. Invention was followed by arrangement and then style; the points of the case were put in the best order, and the appropriate style was determined, depending on the nature of the appeal and the audience. Memory and delivery finished the job: An orator memorized his speech and perfected the delivery.

Memory, as I understood it, referred to the act of memorization, not an art but a skill—the skill of recall, useful to ancient orators but made obsolete by writing and the printing press and computer technology. Edward P. J. Corbett's *Classical Rhetoric for the Modern Student* stated the prevailing attitude well: "after rhetoric came to be concerned mainly with written discourse, there was no further need to deal with memorizing" (27), and Corbett dismissed memory from his text.

My understanding, I've since concluded, was incomplete. Studying classical western rhetoric shows that most rhetorical scholars and thinkers give memory much more status than I did, or than Corbett did. Even when the ancient orator/philosophers defined the canon of memory as memorization, they also discussed importance of memory as a storehouse of knowledge. The more an orator knew—the more knowledge and experience he had stored in his head—the better he would be able to invent appropriate arguments and convince his audiences through an effective style and delivery. Memory in this sense precedes invention and becomes the source of inventive possibilities. This view of memory was held by both Plato and Aristotle.

Historically, memory has been considered an important rhetorical faculty and an art, not just a skill for memorizing speeches. This art involves the full range of the intellect, including both imagination and reasoning; it is not mere rote learning. Many early rhetoricians and philosophers believed memory to be the origin of all knowledge, the base on which understanding rests. Often, they treat it as a creative and constructive force, generating the ideas and the forms that become the written product.

This book is for those who study rhetoric, who write, and who teach writing. In it, I urge you to give memory an acknowledged place throughout the rhetorical or composing process rather than a now meaningless place at the end. The book should accomplish three goals. The first is to supply readers with a clear picture of the history of memory in rhetoric and of contemporary approaches to memory in our own discipline and in others. The second is to persuade readers to elevate the status of memory to that of a vital canon of contemporary rhetoric critical to the formation of both forms and ideas. The final goal is to convince readers that developing a revised theory of memory goes hand in hand with respect for a *variety* of rhetorics and arms us against a technological future in which individual and cultural differences might be erased.

In his 1993 book, *History as an Art of Memory*, Patrick H. Hutton calls memory "the quintessential interdisciplinary interest" (xiii). He's right. The study of memory respects no boundaries. As I searched for information about memory's role in rhetoric, I found myself in so many fields that I was almost overwhelmed. One find led to another, and another, and soon the whole written history of humanity seemed to be heaped at my feet, in pieces. I picked up some of those pieces, gingerly at first, adding to my knowledge the musings and meditations and scientific experiments of others. These fragments are like pottery shards, glued together here in a new shape. They fit together in a way that makes memory an essential part of rhetoric. By looking at other fields we can begin to appreciate just how greatly the making of knowledge depends on memory.

Enlarging the definition of memory is much like climbing to the roof to look at the lay of the land from a panoramic perspective. It is one more way to view the territory. It is not necessarily a new way: Memory has been given broad powers by scholars throughout history and across disciplines. A broader view of memory is useful for understanding how we interpret life and for improving how we write about it.

Reviewing the histories of rhetoric and composition against contemporary knowledge in psychology, philosophy, and literature, I believe that the following statements about memory can be made:

- Memory is a key component of rhetoric—the mother of our muses, the storehouse of all our knowledge.
- Memory generates knowledge as well as preserving it. Through memory we reconstruct our past experience and make new knowledge.

- Memory is based on both our individual and our social histories. The knowledge it provides us reflects experiences at the personal, societal, and universal levels of our existence.
- Memory is activated by innumerable stimuli, from visual images to smells to words. This fact becomes important as our vehicles of communication and storage change. We must ask if the means of remembering affects the kinds of knowledge we make from those memories.
- Memory thus defined sparks the human imagination and kindles inspiration and discovery. From memory comes the muse that inspires us to regenerate ideas and discover new connections and, therefore, write.
- *Memoria*, the thing remembered, is all we have. Upon memory rests our ability to think, speak, and write.

It is this far more complex idea of memory that has potential to influence teachers, students, and writers. We look to other fields and our own for answers to important questions: How does memory work and what part does it play in the writing process? How does it determine what we absorb, what we think, what we write and how we structure our ideas? How does memory help us retrieve the past and connect experience and ideas? What happens in the memories of our readers, listeners, and students as they receive our messages and interpret them?

These questions are explored in the following chapters. The answers, I believe, prove that memory is an essential part of rhetoric, and that recognizing it as such will influence our pedagogy as teachers and our own processes as writers.

Memory is important not only as a source of individual expression, but as a source of cultural expression as well. Cultural memory allows us to discern, express, and value differences based on gender, race, and social background.

This cultural or social memory can link us to our roots and our future, can cultivate a variety of rhetorics and can work as a defense against sameness and inequality. Kathleen Welch defines the centrality of memory to cultural expression: She states that when memory and delivery were removed from rhetoric, we lost rhetoric's relation to our culture. Invention, style, and arrangement can exist in a vacuum, she says; it is memory and delivery that connect us to "history, culture, and the life of the polis" ("The Platonic Paradox" 9). In other words, it takes a complete rhetoric—one that includes both memory and delivery—to promote and change our culture(s).

One of the most compelling reasons for studying memory is the change our technological society forces on our ideas of memory and language, change as great as the alphabet and the printing press in their times. External sources of memory have multiplied—libraries, databases, and videotapes—creating new questions about the nature of individual and collective memory. What is the value of the individual memory in a world that chronicles so readily what we all should remember? What forces in our culture determine what collective memories we will have? Advertisers? Television producers? Politicians? Teachers? These questions lead to possible answers that are both exciting and frightening. George Orwell's *1984* is a novel of forced forgetting. Today we find ourselves more vulnerable than

Orwell ever imagined to sophisticated database manipulation and mass media culturization. What might we be forced to remember and to forget? I imagine how different our knowledge about the Holocaust would be without Anne Frank's *The Diary of a Young Girl*, and I speculate about other perspectives we have not been able to read. We always need someone to record major events from an unofficial point of view.

Too, external means of storage, though in one sense more permanent than our minds, are in another way ossified, disposable, replaceable, manipulable. A tape melts in the sun on the dashboard of the car; we record over a movie when a better one comes along. And in external forms of storage, the originals are not re-collected or influenced by later events; they are as before, which may not be as we need them now. The important connections, those that can be rearranged and reassessed, are still, and only, in our heads.

The Structure of This Book

The following chapters discuss memory in the history of rhetoric, in psychology, in philosophy, in literature, and in rhetoric and composition studies. Chapter 2 looks at the history of memory as a canon of rhetoric, from its "invention" by Simonides in the 5th century BC to its virtual demise in the 18th century. The history of memory is a surprisingly interesting study. Few books have been written about it; the classic *The Art of Memory* by Francis Yates, written in 1966, stood alone for years as the definitive work on the subject. Yet the history of memory is a fascinating study that links rhetoric to philosophy, to magic, to literature, to psychology, to the nature of knowledge itself.

Chapters 3, 4, and 5 move from the field of rhetoric to contemporary psychology, philosophy, and literature. The work of researchers in these disciplines illustrates the links between memory, creation, creativity, and communication. We see rhetoric as a force that derives from memory—we invent what we have to say from what is in our memories, which is what we know. Rhetoric shapes our thought and our culture, too. How we speak and write influences how information is remembered; it affects how we interpret our world.

Several memory "constants" are acknowledged across the disciplines. One is that memory is truly a storehouse of knowledge, just as early rhetoricians like Plato and Cicero suggested. A second is that memory does more than just store knowledge; it creates knowledge as well, constantly adding to itself and reconstructing its contents. To see memory as a source that creates knowledge is to see it as a source of both understanding and inspiration. A third shared belief is that memory is almost unlimited in what it can hold and that we are not conscious of much that it does hold. The most enigmatic workings of memory occur at the unconscious level. Researchers in social psychology and philosophers even suggest that some of the memory traces we possess come from ancestral patterns and precede our own births. A fourth belief shared in psychology, philosophy, and literature is that memory and language are inextricably related. The relationship is as complicated as that between the chicken and the egg. Memory allows us to store language, yet language seems to be the vehicle through which we keep experience. Fifth, studies relating to memory in psychology, philosophy, and literature emphasize the social nature of the construction, retention, and reconstruction of knowledge. How and what we remember and think are dependent on when and where we live. Even our memories are formed by the world around us.

These shared beliefs about memory are the basis for suggesting that a study of memory belongs in rhetoric and in the writing classroom. If memory not only stores but creates knowledge, if knowledge must come from what we have experienced, if language and memory enhance one another so that remembering and writing work dialectically, and if speaking and writing are inevitably guided by cultural experience and expectations, then memory may be the strongest yet least appreciated influence on a student who tries to write. *Memory is a powerful tool readily available to every writer.*

Chapter 6 looks at the study of memory in rhetoric and composition and considers how this powerful tool might enhance our understanding of rhetoric and our ability to write and to teach writing. New research and practices in rhetoric and composition theory in the last 25 years show how important a factor memory is in the generation of ideas and of writing.

Teaching students to think about and value memory as a part of the rhetorical process will help them to improve their writing. Individual writers will become more confident, more interesting, and more "true" as writers, by understanding the ties between past and present, and by seeing the connection between their personal lives, their cultures, and their language. But writing will improve in even more significant ways, as chapter 7 demonstrates. Valuing memory allows writers to break from the bonds of traditional practices. It allows them to break out of conventions and to write themselves.

Valuing memory not only acknowledges and allows rhetorics that are different or marginalized, it validates and encourages them. Chapter 7 describes how important memory is to the rhetorics of "other" cultures—Chinese, Native American, feminist, and others. Mainstream American culture works in marked contrast—we seem to disparage the past (our cultures, our memories, our experience) and look only to the future. However, in an age of rapid technological change, when the voices and images of television influence most Americans daily, it is crucial that we understand how our thoughts and our memories are shaped by the mass culture. We must learn both how to use and how to defy that culture if we are to create and to pass on powerful ideas through powerful language. Powerful language is memorable language; it binds speaker and listener, writer and reader in shared experience. It does not limit thought; it expands it.

This book represents the expansion of my own thought and my own memory—my reconstruction of reality—as I begin to understand both the confines and the possibilities of the social worlds I inhabit and the language I use. My memory is not only fuller than it was before; it is changed.

Chapter 2

Memory and the History of Rhetoric

Musings

Denver, Colorado has a lovely Center for the Performing Arts. It includes a 3,000-seat theater, which opened in November 1991 with Phantom of the Opera. I was there with my family, only a few short weeks after it opened. Our seats were in the very last row.

Now we didn't know our seats would be in the back row until we arrived and found our places. We chuckled and scratched our heads as we peered miles down to the stage. What else could we do? We had ordered the least expensive tickets. The good news was that the very back row (and, except for the boxes, only the very back row) had moveable armchairs for seats. Perhaps we were lucky to be sitting there. So we rented some opera glasses, rested our arms on the railing in front of us, and, once the music began, forgot about the distance between us and the spellbinding drama below.

Imagine what the theater must look like from the stage! Come with me. Let's walk down there and look out—at the orchestra pit, at the orchestra seats, at the geometric boxes hanging from the walls, at the mezzanine, the balconies, and—way, way up there—that last row of moveable chairs. Then look straight up at the battens for the lights and the scenery, and look into the wings, to the stage doors; from here we can see the real workings of the theater that create the magic we saw from out there.

Stretch your imagination even farther. We're still standing on the stage, but now we're not looking around in Denver's new theater, but in your memory. And all the seats out front and all the storage spaces in back are filled with your life. Your mother is in one of the boxes, still worrying about you after 40 years. In the orchestra pit you find the stream you fished in as a kid, the one you've been longing to find again, and you find Women in Love, the book that turned you into an English major. A few seats behind the book sits Professor Milter, the guy who ruined poetry for you until you fell in love with the poet who wrote just for you. The loneliness you felt when that ended is up there on your right. And in the balcony are the words to all the songs from the 1960s that you can still belt out by heart.

Behind and above you is Uncle Mort's vicious laugh. It can still raise the hair on your neck even though you haven't heard it in 25 years. The scent of Chanel No. 5 floats from the wings of your adolescence; behind you lurk your son's hugs, before he got too old to hug.

Look up to that back row, where I sat for Phantom, and you might see nothing, or you might see phantoms of your own, whisking darkly among themselves, indistinguishable. But hold up opera glasses, and look closely. Over on your left, if you try very hard, you might be able to pick out all the kings and queens of England, in order. You knew every one of them in seventh grade, remember? Now take those empty seats down front, and fill them with your new class' names and faces, so you can say "Good morning, Don" and "Hi, Jan" on the second day of class. Try it; you can do it.

Sometimes I wish the theater of my memory was just a tiny place, with room for only what I want to keep. Other times I think I require a stadium for all that I need to know. Usually, however, the balance seems to go the other way: I have a stadium full of phantoms from the past, and only a closet's worth of useful knowledge.

* * *

A great and beautiful invention is memory, always useful both for learning and for life. (Simonides, *Dialexis*, c.400 BC, qtd. in Yates, *Art* 29)

The nine muses were born on the northern face of Mount Olympus, the daughters of Zeus and Mnemosyne, or Memory. Mnemosyne's parentage was distinguished; she was the daughter of Heaven and Earth. The nine muses represent all the graces of civilization: epic poetry, history, lyric and love poetry, music, choral dance and song, tragedy, comedy, sacred poetry, and astronomy. The muses drank from the springs of Mt. Pierus, and these waters were the inspiration for their arts. Although poets throughout time have "drunk from the Pierian spring" for inspiration, originally the Muses served a purpose more functional than inspirational: Without writing, it was the Muses who would preserve tradition. They spoke of things of "the present and the before" and also of "the to become" (Havelock 80). Their parentage—Zeus and Memory—made them "the guardians of the social memory" (Havelock 79). But the Muses have always been thought to inspire. They "cause the soul to remember its forgotten higher estate" (Campbell 104). Throughout history artists have invoked the muse, and many of us who write beg frequently for divine inspiration.

The muse that we invoke, then, and the muse our students invoke, is a direct descendant of Memory. However, in the classic rhetorical sense, memory takes on a narrower definition. Memory was taught as one of the five canons of rhetoric, along with invention, style, arrangement, and delivery. It was the ability to memorize, the tricks that allowed orators to remember their speeches.

Memory involves a great deal more than the memorization of speeches, however. Memory plays a much more vital role in rhetoric, whether written or spoken. This role can be based on some of the broader classic definitions of memory that the discipline of rhetoric seems to have forgotten.

Memory in Classical Rhetoric

The "discovery" of memory is credited to Simonides, who lived about 400 BC. According to the story, Simonides was at a large banquet and was called to the door by two strangers. While he was outside, the ceiling of the banquet hall caved in. Everyone else was killed, and the bodies were crushed beyond recognition. Simonides, however, realized that he could identify all the victims because he could remember where each was sitting. Thus he realized that by remembering places (loci) he could remember "things" (images), the people at the banquet (Yates, *Art* 3). Simonides' discovery led to serious efforts to develop the power of the memory. A good memory was particularly important for orators, whose oratorical prowess depended on the ability to memorize their speeches.

The "narrow" definition of memory as memorization that survives in most rhetoric texts comes from classical works that explain the art of memorization necessary for orators. Nowhere is memory explained as clearly as in the *Rhetorica Ad Herennium*, a work of uncertain authorship written about 84 BC which served for centuries as the basis of understanding memory as a part of rhetoric.

Because the *Ad Herennium* contains such a complete definition of memory, it is a good place to begin. Then we can look at some of the works that preceded and followed it, sharing its narrow definition of memory as a canon of rhetoric. We can then compare it to some other classical descriptions of memory that take a broader view of memory, defining it as the source of knowledge and inspiration, as in the classical myth, identifying memory as the mother of the muses.

The *Rhetorica Ad Herennium* sets out the five canons of rhetoric—invention, arrangement, style, memory, and delivery—with memory consisting of the mnemonics and practice necessary to assure accurate delivery. It describes memory at length. Because it provides the most complete and influential classical definition, it is worth looking at a long segment of it here:

> Now let me turn to the treasure-house of the ideas supplied by Invention, to the guardian of all the parts of rhetoric, the Memory.
>
> ... There are, then, two kinds of memory: one natural, and the other the product of art. The natural memory is that memory which is imbedded in our minds, born simultaneously with thought. The artificial memory is that memory which is strengthened by a kind of training and system of discipline. But just as in everything else the merit of natural excellence often rivals acquired learning, and art, in its turn, reinforces and develops the natural advantages, so does it happen in this instance. The natural memory, if a person is endowed with an exceptional one, is often like this artificial

memory, and this artificial memory, in its turn, retains and develops the natural advantages by a method of discipline. Thus the natural memory must be strengthened by discipline so as to become exceptional, and, on the other hand, this memory provided by discipline requires natural ability. It is neither more nor less true in this instance than in the other arts that science thrives by the aid of innate ability, and nature by the aid of the rules of art. The training here offered will therefore also be useful to those who by nature have a good memory, as you will yourself soon come to understand. But even if these, relying on their natural talent, did not need our help, we should still be justified in wishing to aid the less well-endowed. Now I shall discuss the artificial memory.

The artificial memory includes backgrounds and images. By backgrounds I mean such scenes as are naturally or artificially set off on a small scale, complete and conspicuous, so that we can grasp and embrace them easily by the natural memory—for example, a house, an intercolumnar space, a recess, an arch, or the like. An image is, as it were, a figure, mark, or portrait of the object we wish to remember; for example, if we wish to recall a horse, a lion, or an eagle, we must place its image in a definite background. Now I shall show what kind of backgrounds we would invent and how we should discover the images and set them therein. (205–209)

The explanation goes on:

those who have learned mnemonics can set in backgrounds what they have heard, and from these backgrounds deliver it by memory. For the backgrounds are very much like wax tablets or papyrus, the images like the letters, the arrangement and disposition of the images like the script, and the delivery is like the reading. We should, therefore, if we desire to memorize a large number of items, equip ourselves with a large number of backgrounds, so that in these we may set a large number of images ... (209)

The image of the memory as a waxen tablet upon which inscriptions are written is the most persistent image to come down to us from classical times. The other constant image is the one that begins the memory section quoted here—memory as a storehouse of knowledge. These images are important to a broadened definition of memory, as explained in the next section of this chapter, for they show that memory is connected to writing (written images on a waxen tablet) and to knowledge (the storehouse of knowledge).

The next few pages of the memory section in the *Ad Herennium* suggest ways to organize the backgrounds in which the items to be memorized will be placed. Once the background structure is created, the orator fills its rooms with images that represent the parts of the speech. Thus, if I am an orator preparing a speech, I create a mansion inside my head, plan my rooms, and decorate them, and when I have a speech to memorize, I simply put one part of my speech into every room. As I mentally go from room to room in a logical, designated order, I will remember the contents of each room, thereby flawlessly remembering my speech.

The *Ad Herennium* discusses the "theory of images" (213): a person can conjure up both likenesses of subject matter (the main points) and likenesses of words. A single image can remind us of a complete idea, but it takes many images to remember many words—so remembering word by word is the more difficult task of memorization. We can make memorizing easier by being "novel" or "marvellous" (219), for striking images are more likely to be remembered.

Quickly the treatise moves on to delivery, the last part of rhetoric, without ever telling the reader exactly how to perform these memory feats. Nowhere in the extant literature do we get explicit instructions; we must assume that if there were specific pedagogical techniques for building the memory, the teachers of oratory knew what they were and had their students practice them.

From its beginnings, the study of memory is referred to as an art. We might be tempted to think that training the memory to memorize is more of a skill than an art, but the classic rhetoricians deemed it a true art, the mastery of which took time, effort, imagination, and a good mind.

Along with the *Ad Herennium*, the works of Cicero and Quintilian are the important Roman sources of information about memory as a canon of rhetoric. Of the two, Cicero gives more emphasis to the art of memory, using a five-part system of rhetoric like that outlined in the *Rhetorica Ad Herennium*. This was first set out in *De Inventione*, probably written about the same time as the *Ad Herennium*. (In fact, for centuries Cicero was thought to be the author of that document, too.) Apparently by that time (around 84 BC) the five-part system was a common method for teaching rhetoric (Bizzell and Herzberg 195). Later in *De Oratore* (written about 54 BC), Cicero again defines the art, giving a rather extensive explanation of the workings and advantages of memory training. His conception of memory is like that in the *Ad Herennium*; he too stresses the use of places and things, and he suggests the waxen tablet metaphor for memory. He does add that the effectiveness of memory training depends on a person's natural ability. But he believes that no one's natural memory is so strong or so weak that it can't be improved by training.

Quintilian defines memory and describes ways to improve it in the 11th book of *Institutio Oratorio*, published in 95 AD. He too believes firmly that a good trained memory is a necessity for an orator:

> For while we are saying one thing, we must be considering something else that we are going to say: consequently, since the mind is always looking ahead, it is continually in search of something which is more remote: on the other hand, whatever it discovers, it deposits by some mysterious process in the safe-keeping of memory, which acts as a transmitting agent and hands on to the delivery what it has received from the imagination. (213–215)

His system differs from the *Rhetorica Ad Herennium* and from Cicero in that he does not hold much stock in a visual memory system that relies on "places" and "things." He instead argues for straight text memorization, and therefore gives us the basis of most memorization practices used in schools throughout Western history: "The most important thing is to learn much by heart and to think much, and, if possible, to do this daily, since there is nothing that is more increased by practice or impaired by neglect than memory ..." (236).

The systems of memory exemplified by Cicero and Quintilian fixed memory's place in the background of our current rhetorical landscape, and memory became even less important as writing replaced oratory as the focus of rhetoric. When a speaker could write down what he wanted to say, he didn't need such a good memory. And when he was no longer a speaker at all but a writer whose works were just read, memorization was useless.

However, Cicero and Quintilian were not the only early scholars to think about memory. Many of the classical rhetoricians envisioned a more fundamental role for memory. Their thoughts provide a useful start for redefining memory as an important part of the study of rhetoric today.

Memory as Knowledge

One predecessor in time to the *Ad Herennium* is Plato's *Theaetetus*, which gives us the waxen tablet image later seen in the *Ad Herennium*. Socrates speaks:

> Imagine, then, for the sake of argument, that our minds contain a block of wax, which in this or that individual may be larger or smaller, and composed of wax that is comparatively pure or muddy, and harder in some, softer in others, and sometimes of just the right consistency.

He goes on:

> Let us call it the gift of the Muses' mother, Memory, and say that whenever we wish to remember something we see or hear or conceive in our own minds, we hold this wax under the perceptions or ideas and imprint them on it as we might stamp the impression of a seal-ring. Whatever is so imprinted we remember and know so long as the image remains; whatever is rubbed out or has not succeeded in leaving an impression we have forgotten and do not know. (191 C.–D.: 121)

This waxen tablet image of memory is important for two reasons. First, as *Theaetetus'* translator Francis Cornford suggests, it gives a new meaning to the word *know*: "I know a thing when I have had direct acquaintance with it and an image of it remains stored in my memory" (121). We can easily argue that what we know, then, is what is in our memories: that memory is the place from which *all* knowledge comes, or at least the place where all knowledge is stored. *Knowing is remembering; remembering is knowing.*

A second key point about the waxen tablet image is that it uses writing as a metaphor for memory. Our minds "read" what has been inscribed on the tablet. An interesting fact, though, is that ancient Greek did not have a word meaning "to read"; their word for it (*anagignosko*) means "to recollect," "to know again." The Latin verb is *lego*: "to collect" or "to gather" (Carruthers 30).

"Writing" on the waxen tablet of the mind was one thing; writing on an actual tablet was quite another. Writing was seen by some as a threat to memory and to the educated mind. It was the object of concern and even contempt, just as the computer sometimes is today. In *Phaedrus*, Plato has Socrates argue against writing because it relieves people of having to develop their memories. The external memory—the piece of writing itself—will simply "remind" the reader, which won't lead him to wisdom.

Plato explains the difference in the following passage: Socrates tells Phaedrus of the god Theuth, who brought his invention, writing, to the King of Egypt. But the king tells Theuth:

> You have invented an elixir not of memory, but of reminding; and you offer your pupils the appearance of wisdom, not true wisdom, for they will read many things without instruction and will therefore seem to know many things, when for the most part they are only ignorant and hard to get along with, since they are not wise, but only appear wise. (140)

Wisdom comes from memory. Plato says that by remembering, he can get beyond his own life; he can divine with the gods:

> the mind of the philosopher only has wings, for he is always, so far as he is able, in communion through memory with those things the communion with which causes God to be divine. Now a man who employs such memories rightly is always being initiated into perfect mysteries and he alone becomes truly perfect; but since he separates himself from human interests and turns his attention to the divine, he is rebuked by the vulgar, who consider him mad and do not know that he is inspired. (*Phaedrus* 125)

Plato calls this "divine madness." Joseph Campbell, in *The Masks of God*, argues that the unfolding of many great civilizations was marked by signs of insanity (divine madness?): the pyramids, the royal tombs of Ur, the great cathedrals of the 12th and 13th centuries. He says that these times were mythologically, not economically, inspired (46). If one is "in communion through memory" with God, if he is employing memories to achieve his perfection/madness, he is, apparently, inspired by memory, mother of the Muses.

Plato associates memory with "a dialectical process of shifting gazes" (Covino, *Art* 21). It's "the intellectual capacity for probing the ambiguity of language" (20) or what Plato refers to as "what we assert to be real" that makes us human:

> for to be a man one must understand the content of a general term, leaving the field of manifold sense perceptions, and entering that in which the object of knowledge is unique and grasped only by reasoning. This process is a remembering of what our soul once saw as it made its journey with a god, looking down upon what we now assert to be real and gazing upwards at what is Reality itself. (qtd. in Covino, *Art* 21)

Today we are apt to question Plato's idea of a "Reality itself." We are less apt to believe in an absolute reality, and more apt to believe that the perspective from which each of us gazes creates its own reality. But Plato's views on the ambiguous nature of language and the importance of perspective make it easy to connect him to 20th century rhetorical theory.

Frances Yates believes that, for Plato, memory was not a "part" of rhetoric but "the groundwork of the whole" (Yates, *Art* 37). Plato would have disapproved of learning simplified processes of memory just to remember a speech. In fact, he accused the Sophists of teaching memorization by trivial tricks, whereas Platonic memory involved "knowledge of the truth and of the soul" that "consists in remembering, in the recollection of the Ideas once seen by all souls ..." (Yates, *Art* 36). This broader definition reappears in Renaissance studies of memory and is important today as we consider concepts of cultural and ancestral memory.

For Plato, rhetoric "partakes of the Forms and the soul's attempt through language to have access to them" (Welch, "Platonic" 8). It involves the existence of the past within the present. Even the *Rhetorica Ad Herennium* acknowledges the essential importance of memory, for it is called "the treasure-house of the ideas supplied by Invention ... the guardian of all the parts of memory" (205). Memory in these definitions is no longer a rather limited rhetorical art, but the foundation of and the key to all knowledge.

Aristotle has wonderful words for memory. In *De Memoria et Reminiscentia* (*On Memory*), Aristotle says that memory belongs to the part of the soul "to which imagination also appertains, and all objects of which there is imagination are in themselves objects of memory ..." (715). "Without an image, thinking is impossible," Aristotle states (*De Memoria* 714), and it is memory that collects and stores these images. Memory is a collection of mental pictures from sense impressions with a time element added: "Memory is, therefore, neither perception nor conception, but a state or affection of one of these, conditioned by a lapse of time" (714). Thought works on the stored images of the past, and the intellect is called into play (Yates, *Art* 33). Media and rhetoric critic Bruce Gronbeck believes that *De Memoria et Reminiscentia* is extremely important for how it defines recollection as "the reconstruction of sequences of understanding" (Gronbeck 141). Gronbeck says that unlike the author of the *Ad Herennium*, Aristotle "is grappling with timeless questions about the source of the power of the past" (139).

In *De Anima* Aristotle says that imagination is the intermediary between perception and thought. In other words, knowledge comes from sense impressions after they've been absorbed by the imaginative faculty. It is therefore the image-making part of the soul that makes higher thought processes possible: The soul never thinks without a mental picture (Yates, *Art* 32).

Even Cicero, whose writings on rhetoric are connected most closely with the technical tradition that educated orators and taught them to memorize, realized that knowledge comes from that which we already know, that which is stored in our memories. And this knowledge is the basis of rhetoric:

> the efficacy of the whole of this science, or perhaps I should say pseudoscience, of rhetoric, is not that it wholly originates and engenders something no part of which is already present in our minds, but that it fosters and strengthens things that have already sprung to birth within us. (*De Oratore*, II, lxxxvii, 356: 469)

Early in *De Oratore* Cicero refers to memory as "that universal treasure-house" (I, v., 18: 15). Cicero says that, for an orator, "a knowledge of very many matters" is necessary: knowledge of language and emotions, "humor, culture, flashes of wit," and "the complete history of the past and a store of precedents" (13). He tells us that unless memory "be placed in charge of the ideas and phrases which have been thought out and well weighed ... they will all be wasted" (15). Memory here has the responsibility for safekeeping all knowledge.

Cicero expanded the rhetorician's view of memory by giving it ethical implications. In his discussion of the four virtues (Prudence, Justice, Fortitude, and Temperance), he places memory under Prudence along with intelligence and foresight. Medieval scholars studied memory primarily as a part of prudence; it may have been Ciceronian influence that kept memory alive in medieval Christendom (Yates, *Art* 20).

After the fall of the Roman empire the demand for good public orators declined. The art of memory was preserved primarily through the church for the next 1,000 years, for the art of oratory was still alive in the church. But the interest in memory went beyond simply memorizing sermons. In *On Christian Doctrine*, St. Augustine explains the cleric's need for a good memory to interpret the Scriptures: The more the Scriptures were present in his memory, the more correctly he could interpret (know) them.

St. Augustine is one of many scholars who see memory not as an inscription in wax—a replica—but as a new interpretation. He says in the *Confessions* that there are not past, present, and future as such:

> Perhaps it would be proper to say there are three periods of time: the present of things past, the present of things present, and the present of things future. For these things are in the soul and I do not see them elsewhere: the present of things past is memory. (233)

Does this show his awareness of the constructed nature of the past as it resides in our memory? It appears to do that; thus we can link Augustine and Plato before him to many later philosophers and rhetoricians who believe that the past is a reconstruction of the individual mind. And if that is so, the individual memory is crucial to speaking and writing. External memories like books and libraries may aid us, but the interpretation of reality based on our own memories is the our primary source of wisdom.

In the *Confessions* Augustine describes "The Wonders of Memory" for pages, describing "the fields and broad palaces of memory, where there are treasures of innumerable images brought in from all sorts of sense objects" (8.12: 78). He, like Plato, believed that memory even gives us the power to know God. For him, memory is a part of the trinity of the soul—memory, will, and understanding. These together make up the essence of a person: "And hence these three are one, in that they are one life, one mind, one essence" (*On the Trinity*, 11.18: 77). Memory is knowledge, and it determines our interpretation of and our choices in our world.

Memory and Rhetoric in Medieval Times

The study of memory was kept alive during medieval times by a few scholarly clergymen who made memory a part of their study and used the art to enhance their work. These men accepted memory as a canon of rhetoric, often seeing it, like some predecessors, as the noblest canon (Carruthers 9). Like Cicero, they saw memory as a part of prudence, "that which makes moral judgment possible"; they believed a trained memory helped build "character, judgment, citizenship, and piety" (Carruthers 9). In fact, memory was studied more as a part of logic and moral philosophy than of rhetoric.

Mary Carruthers' *The Book of Memory: A Study of Memory in Medieval Culture* is an excellent resource for studying memory in this period and relating it to both previous and later times. Carruthers calls the society of the middle ages a "memorial" culture, one which assumed the training of the memory to be a natural part of education,

> a matter of ethics. A person without a memory, if such a thing could be, would be a person without moral character and, in a basic sense, without humanity. *Memoria* refers not to how something is communicated, but to what happens once one has received it, to the interactive process of familiarizing—or textualizing—which occurs between oneself and others' words in memory. (13)

She asserts that, for medieval culture, creativity came through having a rich storehouse of knowledge in memory and being able to use it in reconstructed form. Memory is therefore a *foundation* for rhetoric and for life, an important source not only for speaking and writing, but for thinking, too. The trained memory is important so that what one has learned can be retrieved for use. Memory and learning are inseparable. Memory is not just a reproduction but a reconstruction of past experience, a way of making new knowledge.

Memory is also a socializing force. Carruthers suggests that common literary texts (oral or written) can provide the sources for a groups' memory. "Such 'socializing' of literature is the work of *memoria*. ... Whether the words come through the sensory gateways of the eyes or the ears, they must be processed and transformed in memory—they are made our own" (12). *Memoria* was so important to medieval culture, Carruthers believes, that she refers to it as a modality of the culture, like chivalry, "a set of institutionalized practices" that conditioned and thus directed the culture (260). Her view here need not be limited to medieval culture; memory is surely a modality of all cultures, one that conditions and directs them in a multitude of ways.

The two scholars most responsible for keeping the study of memory alive during the Middle Ages were Albertus Magnus and his student Thomas Aquinas. Albertus Magnus wrote on memory in *De Bono* (On the Good), and Aquinas in *Secunda Secundae* of *Summa Theologiae*; they also both wrote commentaries on Augustine's treatise on memory. Both drew on the *Rhetorica Ad Herennium*, but their interest in memory was ethical rather than rhetorical.

Frances Yates explains how memory appears to have been useful to the Dominican friars of the 13th century. First of all, the Dominicans were an order of preachers, and they could use memory training for preaching. Second, memory was important as a part of the virtue of prudence. Cicero had spelled it out hundreds of years earlier in *De Inventione*:

> Prudence is the knowledge of what is good, what is bad and what is neither good nor bad. Its parts are memory, intelligence, foresight. Memory is the faculty by which the mind recalls what has happened. Intelligence is the faculty by which it ascertains what is. Foresight is the faculty by which it is seen that something is going to occur before it occurs. (II, liii,160, qtd. in Yates, *Art* 20)

Mary Carruthers points out that during the Middle Ages, different types of memory systems existed—not just those based on "places" and "images" but systems based on letters and numbers as well (80). However, the systems used by the friars seem to have been based primarily on images, and the more imaginative the images were, the better. What more wonderful way to depict the virtues and vices than through fantastic imagery? Francis Yates conjectures that the use of imagery in the creation of memory structures had a profound influence:

> This inner art which encouraged the use of the imagination as a duty must surely have been a major factor in the evocation of images. Can memory be one possible explanation of the mediaeval love of the grotesque, the idiosyncratic? Are the strange figures to be seen on the pages of manuscripts and in all forms of mediaeval art not so much the revelation of a tortured psychology as evidence that the Middle Ages, when men had to remember, followed classical rules for making memorable images? Is the proliferation of new imagery in the thirteenth and fourteenth centuries related to the renewed emphasis on memory by the scholastics? (*Art* 104)

Yates believes that the answers to these questions may well be "yes." She even makes an interesting suggestion that the landscapes of Dante's *Divine Comedy* may have been based on the architecture of a memory theater, a complex structure housing the places on which images can be remembered. This interpretation suggests *Divine Comedy* might be an example of "how the cultivation of images in the devout uses could have stimulated creative works of art and literature" (96).

The medieval scholars used the memory techniques they had inherited from Greece and Rome. But they used them for more than just the memorization of speeches or sermons, as Yates and Carruthers show: They used them to reconstruct the past and to make new knowledge that helped them make ethical decisions.

What we see in many of these theories of memory is a concern with how we *know*, and a conviction that memory plays a big part in our ability to acquire or create knowledge. That conviction is a basic premise of this book, and it is addressed in more detail later; for now the point is that such a theory has classical roots.

Remembering Through Metaphor

One particular way we can "know" is through the use of metaphor. Before moving on to the Renaissance, it may be useful to look at how classical and medieval rhetoricians perceived metaphor as a part of the rhetorical process. The use of metaphor is an important example of how memory contributes to the making of meaning.

A metaphor is an image, a picture that stirs the brain and conjures up the familiar to give insight to the unfamiliar. A metaphor operates on the memory of the reader or listener: We can only learn something about the object being described if we "know" the qualities of the object to which it is compared. We link what we remember with what we're being told and thus create new knowledge. A successful metaphor touches something recognizable or personal or familiar or common in the listener or reader; it generates meaning.

Throughout history, rhetoricians have spoken of metaphor's value. Aristotle, in the *Poetics,* says "by far the most important thing is to be good at metaphor ... it is a token of high native gifts, for making good metaphors depends on perceiving the likenesses in things" (60–61). He says that metaphor gives so much pleasure because it gives us new knowledge, new perceptions: It bridges the gap between what we know and what we don't know. Cicero, in the *Orator,* tells his students that the only embellishment to use when speaking in plain style is metaphor because all people can understand it; "the borrowing seems to be done to make the meaning clear" (In Benson and Prosser 235). Augustine explains metaphor as one of the ambiguous signs in the third book of *On Christian Doctrine.* In speaking of the tropes in general, he says:

> an awareness of them is necessary to a solution of the ambiguities of the Scriptures, for when the sense is absurd if it is taken verbally, it is to be inquired whether or not what is said is expressed in this or that trope which we do not know, and in this way many hidden things are discovered. (104)

These are just a few early examples of a strong historical interest in metaphor's place in language and in rhetoric.

The key to the success of a metaphor is memory. A metaphor works by tapping common roots of feeling and experience in both the speaker/writer and the audience, by evoking shared knowledge. Although an extended treatise on metaphor would be out of place here, the important point is that metaphor is a way of using language that depends on memory, and its power in speech and writing has been recognized for centuries. Metaphors are examples of social or cultural memory at work: They are examples of how our collective understanding of conventions of language can evoke common images and emotions in a large number of people who share cultural assumptions.

Memory, the Renaissance Era,
and the Occult

Several developments contributed to a waning interest in memory as Europe moved into the Renaissance. The first was the development of the printing press around 1450. With the printed word to "remind" us, as Plato had suggested, there was no longer so much need to memorize. Second was the reappearance of the works of Quintilian. Quintilian's view of memory as a technique solely for memorizing came into favor over the work of Cicero and his followers who categorized memory as a part of Prudence, and the link between memory and ethics was lost. However, the printing press allowed the circulation of many classical texts, and the new humanism promoted other than scholastic methods of using memory.

The interest in memory shifted and narrowed. It lived on in the mystical worlds of Lullism, of cabalism, of hermetic religion, of Neoplatonism, of the occult. An interesting explanation of the difference between the treatment of memory in the Middle Ages and in the Renaissance comes from Yates: Medieval scholars of memory assumed man to be weak; training the memory was a means to make himself a bit better, to improve the imperfect self. Renaissance memory scholars believed man to be divine; the study of memory could take him from his fallen state to a place with God (*Art* 172).

This application of mnemotechnics to achieve a state of divinity came from the ideas of Plato and was popular during the Renaissance as a part of the occult tradition of the times. Serious memory scholars created their own "memory theaters," elaborate structures that were home to the ideas or images or things to be remembered. Some of the most fabulous memory theaters of the time were created by Hermetists, who followed the writings of Hermes Trismegistus of Egypt, probably written between the first and the third centuries AD. Hermetists believe that man can reflect the universe, can understand the divinity of nature. One can know God through contemplation of the world. They believe in the fall of man, but believe that man can reascend by spiritual use of the mind. Through his religious experience, the divinity of his mind can be revealed to him. This journey to understanding takes him through an astrological cosmos, through moons and planets and spheres of angels to the sun.

This journey to truth or knowledge or divinity is reflected in the memory theaters created during the Renaissance. Using the ideas of places and things that the *Rhetorica Ad Herennium* outlined, the "theaters" were actually structures representing the astrological cosmos through which truth could be found. Frances Yates explains in *Giordano Bruno and the Hermetic Tradition*:

> The Hermetic experience of reflecting the universe in the mind is, I believe, at the root of Renaissance magic memory, in which the classical mnemonic with places and images is now understood, or applied, as a method of achieving this experience by imprinting archetypal, or magically activated, images on the memory. By using magical or talismanic images as memory-images, the Magus hoped to acquire

universal knowledge, and also powers, obtaining through the magical organization
of the imagination a magically powerful personality, tuned in, as it were, to the powers
of the cosmos. (191–192)

Take, for example, the memory theater of Guilio Camillo, one of the most
fabulous in the Renaissance. He built his big wooden model in the Hermetic
tradition, and its "secret" was to be told only to the king. In his plan, his theater
rests on the seven pillars of Solomon's House of Wisdom. These pillars represent "stable eternity," and through these he hoped to understand all worlds, right
up to the super-celestial world, and to understand the gods. A person ascends
as his understanding grows. Camillo says, "in order to understand the things of
the lower world it is necessary to ascend to superior things, from whence,
looking down from on high, we may have a more certain knowledge of the
inferior things" (qtd. in Yates, *Art* 143). This idea of shifting gazes is reminis-
cent of Plato in the *Phaedrus*.

The most elaborate and famous of the memory theaters was constructed by
Giordano Bruno, an ex-Dominican who was expelled as a heretic and later
burned at the stake during the Inquisition. The two books already mentioned by
Yates explain his Hermetic beliefs and his elaborate memory system: *Giordano
Bruno and the Hermetic Tradition* and *The Art of Memory*. These definitive
books give excellent background for a reader interested in the art of memory
of the Renaissance mystics. They also give us another perspective on memory,
quite the opposite of the idea of rote memorization that modern rhetoric has
considered its inheritance. They show us an art of memory that stores, seeks,
and creates knowledge.

These memory theaters might aid the rhetorician, too. The orator "might develop
magical powers as an orator by speaking from a memory organically affiliated to
the proportions of the world harmony" (Yates, *Art* 169). The memory of an orator
could be magically activated and the speeches themselves infused with virtues that
would have a magical effect on his audience. "The magic of celestial proportion
flows from his world memory into the magical words of his oratory and poetry, into the
perfect proportions of his art and architecture. Something has happened within the psyche,
releasing new powers ... " (Yates, *Art* 172).

Does any of this relate to us today? There are obvious differences: the
thinkers who kept memory alive in the Renaissance believed in a stable
universe, in the divinity of man, and in absolute truth. Today, when stability,
divinity and truth seem elusive, we might feel that we're on a distant philosophical continent. Yet human knowledge and communication have changed little.
Frances Yates suggests that the important change reflected in Renaissance
thinking was the attitude toward the imagination: "it has become man's highest
power" (*Art* 230). This is the value of the Renaissance art of memory for us: it
is an affirmation of the imaginative powers of humans and a belief that the
memory is the storehouse of those creative powers. As writers and teachers of
writing, we may find that it is by invoking memory that we find our inspiration
and invent what we have to say.

Memory, Ramus, and Print

The isolated mystical groups that kept memory alive during the Renaissance were small in number. Mainstream rhetoric gave little time to memory, although in some cases, a flicker of interest in it remained. Francis Bacon was one scholar who argued for memory's place in rhetoric. In *The Advancement of Learning*, written in 1605, he defines rhetoric this way: "The duty and office of Rhetoric is *to apply Reason to Imagination* for the better moving of the will" (127). He identifies four "Arts Intellectual": Inquiry or Invention, Examination or Judgment, Custody or Memory, and Elocution or Tradition (111).

Memory, he argues, we haven't studied enough: "I find that faculty in my judgment weakly enquired of. An art there is extant of it; but it seemeth to me that there are better precepts than that art, and better practices of that art than those received" (120–121).

However, those influences that reduced memory's role in rhetoric were the stronger influences during the Renaissance era. Two seemingly destructive forces were the influence of Peter Ramus and the growth of the printing industry. But when re-examined, even these emphasize the value of memory.

Peter Ramus' influence on rhetoric in the 16th century was substantial. Ramus was a reformist whose primary aim was to reorganize education in order to simplify it. His work suggests sweeping changes in rhetoric, taking invention, memory and arrangement out of it and leaving only style and delivery—primarily style. The other parts of rhetoric he puts under "dialectic"; his focus for rhetoric is the logical ordering of ideas.

But beyond Ramus' concept of rhetoric lay his philosophy of dialectic, and here he gives memory a place of great importance. Ramus' schemes of arrangement—his concern was the logical ordering of ideas—are really just big memory-based logic systems. He suggests organizing material by starting with universals and moving to the particulars:

> in a great debate which we wish to conduct along straight and orderly lines, the matter in its entirety should be put in the first position and then divided into parts and species; and we should follow to the limit each separate part and its lesser divisions (by proof and explanation) so that the universals go first, and the particulars follow. (114)

Much of his published work is accompanied by tree diagrams in which he illustrates the levels on which he organized his subject matter from generalities to particulars. This logical system has the advantage of "aligning the mind and the material to be known so that they match and bond"; thus it is a perfect and natural memory system (Bizzell and Herzberg 559).

Twentieth-century scholar Walter Ong makes this point in *Ramus, Method, and the Decay of Dialogue*:

> the real reason why Ramus can dispense with memory is that his whole scheme of arts, based on a topically conceived logic, is a system of local memory. Memory is

everywhere, its "places" and "rooms" being the mental space which Ramus' arts all fill. (280)

Rather than treating memory as a factor near the end of the rhetorical process, he makes it the foundation of the entire rhetorical process. His system then substantiates the argument of this book: Memory precedes invention and should be treated as an important first step in the rhetorical process.

Removing invention, arrangement, and memory from rhetoric and making them parts of dialectic or philosophy elevated their importance in his eyes. Yet his legacy for teachers of writing seems to be not his theory of dialectic, but his idea of rhetoric, which is divorced from the generation of ideas and concerned only with style and delivery. Ramus' definition of rhetoric seems a harbinger of what was to come, as we find ourselves 400 years later laden with generations of textbooks that teach writing with an emphasis on stylistic concerns.

The most cited reason for dropping memory from the canons of rhetoric has of course been writing, particularly since the invention of the printing press. Written communication uses a mode of delivery that demands no memorization. Even before we speak, writing allows us to write down what we plan to say: The written words serve as an external memory.

Ong even goes farther in his assessment of printed texts as external memory receptacles. He suggests that the printed products themselves—our books and papers—are memory systems: "the printing form itself [is] a kind of locus, or 'common' place from which can be pulled an unlimited number of printed pages, each blanketed with 'arguments'" (*Ramus* 310). The printer's fonts, the matrices from where they come—these are all storehouses, like memory. Printing is tied up as much in external spatial models as classical memories were in internal models. Perhaps Ong is suggesting that external memory storage from its start is structured in a way that matches our internal need for organization. Perhaps the external memory does not work alone, but by prompting the internal systems with which it must work.

The commonplace books popular in schools during the 16th and 17th centuries served as external memories full of ideas for writing (Calendrillo 63). Students were expected to keep in these copy-books all the ideas of the students in class; thus they would have a greater storehouse of ideas than they could themselves invent (Abbott 114). The problem with these books, Calendrillo suggests, is that the topics become cliches. "Invention through the use of the commonplace books becomes largely a search for apt phrases, not a search for lines of reasoning or intellectually convincing details" (64).

Similarly, we could argue that current-traditional textbooks today that use rhetorical models are storehouses of examples for our imitation. How many students walk into freshman classes "knowing" that a theme for English class has five "places," or paragraphs, and have a sharp "image" of the introduction, the conclusion, and the details and arguments that fit into those five places?

These influences—Ramist rhetoric and the printed word—compel us to recompose our definition of memory. Ramist rhetoric left us a legacy of "rhetoric" as style and delivery, with memory removed from it. The printed word leads us to rely on external memory, replacing the need for a highly developed individual memory. To refute the claim that memory is a dead canon in a literate society, we must acknowledge the generative nature of memory in thought and communication processes. This is the kind of memory that served as the basis for Ramus' "dialectic." And this kind of memory has additional importance for us today when it is easier than ever before to store knowledge externally in new and different forms. At the same time, the more we depend on external sources to remember for us, the more important it becomes to trust our own memory—the true source of our own thinking. Emphasizing memory's place in contemporary rhetoric, writing, and teaching is one way we can encourage the development of the individual memory.

Memory in the Work of Giambattista Vico

Although Giambattista Vico wrote in the early 18th century, he stood outside of accepted Enlightenment thought; he is more like a Renaissance thinker. Although his ideas were not accepted well during his lifetime, his writings are considered much more seriously by contemporary scholars (e.g., see Bizzell and Herzberg or Covino, *Art*). He is an important figure because his concepts of rhetoric support a revised view of rhetoric of which memory is an important part.

Vico opposed Descartes and the scientific method. Vico strongly believed in the value of the imagination and was an early proponent of the idea of a culturally based epistemology (Bizzell and Herzberg 711–712). In his work, Vico criticizes Descartes and his followers for believing that math and science are the only sources of true knowledge; he believes that the knowledge of human affairs—that world which we have created—is the only knowledge available to us. Bizzell and Herzberg summarize Vico's concern in this way:

> What kind of person, what kind of society, will be fostered by Cartesian disdain for the probabilistic knowledge of law, ethics, politics, and medicine? The Cartesian method is useful, Vico concedes, but it cannot be allowed to overpower the kind of commonsense that is stimulated by the study of eloquence, with its appeals to imagination and memory and its practice in the commonplaces of argument. (711)

This common sense he calls "prudence"; he thinks we must teach prudence and ethics, which are based on common sense, or experience, rather than abstract knowledge (*On the Study Methods of Our Time* 720).

The New Science is Vico's major work on rhetoric, and in it we find his ideas on the role of memory in the making of knowledge. Like Aristotle, he states that the human mind can't understand anything of which it has no earlier sense impression. Vico says this is true of the human race in general. He "believes in the power of collective and cultural memory" and "seeks to define a collective mythology to impart a cultural and intellectual heritage" (Calendrillo 81). Memory is the source of both personal and cultural knowledge.

The beginning of knowledge came from the early sages, or "theological poets." The first metaphysics, he says, were not rational and abstract but felt and imagined. The fields of understanding that derived from these metaphysics—logic, morals, economics, and politics—he calls "poetic."

Vico believes that poetic thinking is based in imagination, or memory. Early speech was expressed in fables, or myths—imaginative thinking. A metaphor is "a fable in brief" (404: 129) which explains imaginatively what couldn't be explained as well abstractly or literally. Our first knowledge, then, comes through poetic language, through the powers of imagination. In fact, Vico explains, *logos* (logic) first meant *fabula* (fable) and then became the Italian *favella* (speech) (*New Science*, 401: 127); thus, he suggests the relationship of memory to all thinking.

By emphasizing the value of imagination in human understanding, Vico acknowledges the importance of memory, for to him imagination is part of memory:

> Memory thus has three different aspects: memory when it remembers things, imagination when it alters or imitates them, and invention when it gives them a new turn or puts them into proper arrangement or relationship. (819: 313)

Memory, imagination, discovery, invention, knowledge—all these are integrally related in Vico's system. Creativity, imagination and invention are founded on memory and give rise to knowledge. Again, memory is seen as the source of all we know. William Covino assesses Vico's definition for a modern understanding of memory in this way:

> Memory reconsidered in its Vichian associations becomes an element that cannot be dismissed from a modern, generative rhetoric. Memory is not merely the replication of experience; it is for Vico experience imagined and invented, altered and arranged, recollected and re-associated; it is the foundation of Montaigne's patchwork. Memory is a faculty that makes experience. (*Art* 62)

Memory is the source of ideas. Vico, like Plato and others before him, see memory as a vital rhetorical art which has not just utility but generative powers as well. From memory comes our personal and cultural knowledge; through memory, knowledge is remembered, reconstructed, and reorganized. This is the process through which knowledge is created.

Memory in the Enlightenment and After

The scientific and philosophical revolutions of the Enlightenment, which occurred in the 17th, 18th, and 19th centuries, questioned the concepts on which the world had been based, and so demanded changing attitudes toward rhetoric. The Enlightenment was an age interested in psychology, in the workings not only of the universe but of the mind. John Locke called the mind a blank slate on which experience writes. This description provokes a comparison with the waxen tablet image of classical rhetoricians. For Locke, knowledge comes partly from the experience and partly from reflection on it. Reflection comes from *associating* or making connections between ideas. David Hume and others added to the principle of association: The past is recalled by memory and reinforced by imagination, which results in the making of inferences. Enlightenment thinkers were concerned with the origin of knowledge, and the empiricists, including Locke and Hume, argued that knowledge comes from experience and reflection. They were interested in modern science, in finding truth through experiment.

Locke's vision of the mental process was essentially mechanistic. Put in modern terms, "the mind is like a computer with data inputs (the senses), an informational storage/retrieval system, and some very simple programs, endlessly iterated, to process and compare the data" (Richter 300). Hume moves away from a mechanistic view, as Covino relates:

> Our thinking has form insofar as we link ideas according to both custom and imagination. Certain trains of thought, reinforced by experience and custom, produce matters of fact; but each mind has the power, and the responsibility, to reconsider matters taken for granted and recombine ideas in fresh ways. (*Art* 74)

Locke and Hume perhaps represent the two ends of empirical thought, Locke believing there is a place for reason and Hume finding no room for it. But both suggest an epistemological approach to knowledge which naturally includes consideration of memory, the source of reflection and recollection. Both Locke and Hume influenced philosophical thought as well as rhetoric, and more will be said about them in a later chapter.

The 18th century rhetoricians who most influenced the teaching of rhetoric in England and the United States were George Campbell, Hugh Blair, and Richard Whately. The books of Campbell and Blair were particularly popular in the universities; they were primarily guides to style that emphasized perspicuity—clear language expressing clear thought. Blair and Campbell were interested in the human mind—they were strongly influenced by the philosophy and psychology of their time. They were concerned not just with persuasion but with understanding as well. They believed that invention comes from genius, and therefore they rejected topics and commonplaces as artificial. They accepted Locke's and Hume's philosophical and psychological theories about the association of ideas and the importance of feelings to understanding (Golden and Corbett 15–16).

Blair, Campbell, and Whately do not consider memory as a canon of rhetoric. Whateley does not discuss memory at all in *Elements of Rhetoric* (in Golden and Corbett, 277–399). Blair make a few references to it in *Lectures on Rhetoric and Belles Lettres* (in Golden and Corbett, 28–137). Some of his references treat memory as an organizational aid. He encourages speakers to outline their material (Golden and Corbett 102) and to divide sermons into "heads" (113) as memory aids for both themselves and their listeners. And Blair, like the classical scholars, sees "a fund of knowledge" as second only to moral qualities as a necessity for a good speaker (131).

But Blair mentions memory in a more generative sense, especially as the provocation of memory produces responses in the reader. He recognizes that tropes have value in writing because of their ability to produce associations, recalling more to our memory (77). He encourages the "pathetic" as an essential part of discourse, "in which, if anywhere, eloquence reigns, and exerts its power" (122). In his argument for using pathetic appeals to rouse the passions, he says:

> The foundation ... of pathetic oratory is to paint the object of that passion which we wish to raise ... to awaken it in the minds of others. Every passion is most strongly excited by sensation. ... Next to the influence of sense, is that of memory; and next to memory, is the influence of the imagination. (124)

This argument appears to be a clear plea to consider audience and an assumption that invoking memory is a key to connecting with that audience.

George Campbell refers to memory throughout the first book of *The Philosophy of Rhetoric*. He calls memory "the great luminary of the mind" (Golden and Corbett 218). His comments on memory revolve around two ideas. The first is that all we know personally is based on sensation, which is recorded in memory and which leads to experience as facts remembered are compared (185). Even if our memories are inaccurate, they are critical to knowledge, and we can often correct inaccuracies through experience. But "if we had not previously given an implicit faith to memory, we had never been able to acquire experience" (191). The larger experience that we get about the world from others, Campbell says, is based on "testimony in concurrence with memory" (192). In other words, outside information still has to fuse with what we do know to become our knowledge.

The second way Campbell discusses memory is with respect to audience. In considering the effects of a work on an audience, he believes that four powers, "understanding, imagination, memory, and passion are equally subservient" (208). Conviction, he says, is not possible without memory as an aid to making connections. A speaker will only convince his audience if he uses these four powers to evoke a response in them.

For both Blair and Campbell, then, memory is, in the classical sense, a storehouse of knowledge necessary to experience and understand the world and crucial to produce a response in an audience. Generation of experience, ideas, and conviction depends on memory.

The ideas from the 17th and 18th centuries that most naturally fit with those of the late 20th century are the ideas of the skeptics of the time, thinkers like Montaigne, Vico, and Hume, who "resisted a positivistic epistemology that exalted knowledge-as-information" (Covino, *Art* 79). Despite the breadth of Blair's and Campbell's works, their real popularity was as rule makers. The mainstream teaching of rhetoric, based on the works of Blair, Campbell, Whately, and later Alexander Bain and others, emphasized organization and style. This practice grew through the 19th century and led to a whole discipline of rhetoric based on rules, form, and style.

The prescriptive orientation of those who followed Blair, Campbell, and Whately marked a separation from classical rhetorical studies. This approach has continued to be the main mode of teaching writing; even today, this "current-traditional rhetoric" thrives in many high schools, colleges, and universities. The most complete history or "deconstruction" of current-traditional rhetoric is Sharon Crowley's *The Methodical Memory: Invention in Current-Traditional Rhetoric*. She explains some of the problems inherent to writing instruction as it has been practiced by current-traditionalists.

Crowley's concern is the omission of invention from the teaching of writing. To the new rhetoricians, a good mind "worked in an organized linear sequence" and "the mind's sequential workings were accurately inscribed in memory and could be accurately reproduced on demand" (12). Crowley suggests that invention became a forgotten canon in the teaching of school writing because writing instructors assumed that the creation of a well-organized mind was unteachable. If a student did not have such mental powers, too bad. If she did, then she did not need instruction in using it; she would invent the ideas for her essay easily. The memory and the inventive process were as stiff and predictable as the formal outline of which current-traditional advocates are so fond. Creativity, discovery, and thought took a back seat to formulaic ideas about form and style.

Rhetoric itself withered as a respected teaching subject as well as the foundation of writing instruction. Not until the last 20 years, with the revival of rhetoric and the blossoming of the field of composition studies, can we see our own field beginning to recognize the importance of memory for invention and for writing in general. These contemporary views are discussed in chapter 6.

Memory and the Romantics

The poets made all the words, and therefore language is the archives of history, and, if we must say it, a sort of tomb of the muses. (Ralph Waldo Emerson "The Poet," in Richter 364)

To find an environment that values imagination and memory in writing during the 18th and 19th century, we must look not to rhetoric but to literature, particularly to the Romantics. Bizzell and Herzberg suggest that before romanticism, literature and rhetoric could co-exist compatibly. Literature was instructive and moralistic; criticism made judgments based on rules.

Both rhetoric and criticism operated empirically in an empirical age, examining successful works and identifying the features that made them effective; both relied on classical works as models of enduring effectiveness; and both defined human nature as the general experience of humankind. (665)

The focus of romantic literature was different. Rather than being active and audience-oriented, it was contemplative and author-oriented. It is sometimes considered "antirhetorical" (Bizzell and Herzberg 666). Yet it is only when we define the word *rhetorical* in the very narrowest sense that romanticism can be called "antirhetorical."

Romanticism is expressive—it champions the individual mind, and individual experience becomes the focus of its art. To the romantics, imagination and personal experience are superior to reason, as are spontaneity and subjectivity. Romantics are interested in the past, particularly the mythical past. Historian Patrick Hutton links Romanticism with Vichian uses of memory; memory is "a technique to uncover forgotten origins understood as lost poetic powers" ("Art" 380). It is the romantic belief in the essential importance of the poetic powers, or the imagination, that makes Romanticism a crucial part of a study of memory.

Samuel Taylor Coleridge defines imagination in the 13th chapter of *Biographia Literaria*, published in 1817. The imagination has two parts:

> The primary Imagination I hold to be the living power and prime agent of all human perception, and as a repetition in the finite mind of the eternal act of creation in the infinite I AM. The secondary Imagination I consider as an echo of the former, co-existing with the conscious will, yet still as identical with the primary in the *kind* of its agency, and differing only in *degree*, and in the *mode* of its operation. It dissolves, diffuses, dissipates, in order to recreate: or where this process is rendered impossible, yet still at all events it struggles to idealize and to unify. It is essentially *vital*, even as all objects (*as* objects) are essentially fixed and dead. (159–160)

Coleridge distinguishes Imagination from Fancy:

> Fancy, on the contrary, has no other counters to play with, but fixities and definites. The fancy is indeed no other than a mode of memory emancipated from the order of time and space; while it is blended with, and modified by that empirical phenomenon of the will, which we express by the word Choice. But equally with the ordinary memory the Fancy must receive all its materials ready made from the law of association. (160)

For Coleridge, Fancy is the more limited: it can come up with an idea or image at will, but it cannot recombine or recreate. This most important activity, re-creation, is the job of the secondary imagination—the ability to dissolve, diffuse and dissipate in order to recreate. It is this activity that Coleridge calls "vital."

Coleridge's primary imagination, where perception and creation take place, is much like Immanuel Kant's productive imagination: As *noumena* (things of the external world) hit our senses, our minds turn them into representations or images. We process them by space, time, quality, quantity, substance, and so on, and we end up with phenomena, the world as we see it. We do not just find the phenomenological world in front of us, we create it (Richter 300–301).

The representations of images so created will then be stored in our memories, to be recombined with new experience. Thus those images stored in our memories are basic to the very active process of re-creation, or invention.

William Wordsworth's Preface to *Lyrical Ballads* is the source of his famous definition of poetry based on recollection and contemplation—jobs for memory:

> poetry is the spontaneous overflow of powerful feelings: it takes its origin from emotion recollected in tranquillity; the emotion is contemplated till by a species of reaction the tranquillity gradually disappears, and an emotion, kindred to that which was before the subject of contemplation, is gradually produced, and does itself actually exist in the mind. In this mood successful composition generally begins, and in a mood similar to this it is carried on. (295)

Three points made by Wordsworth in the Preface seem particularly interesting as they relate to memory. One is Wordsworth's justification for using the experiences and the language of the common man. He tells us that "low and rustic life" affords him better opportunity to explain "the essential passions of the heart," for

> in that condition of life our elementary feelings co-exist in a state of greater simplicity, and, consequently, may be more accurately contemplated, and more forcibly communicated ... (288)

The language of the common man, he says,

> arising out of repeated experience and regular feelings, is a more permanent, and a far more philosophical language than that which is frequently substituted for it by poets, who think that they are conferring honor upon themselves and their art, in proportion as they separate themselves from the sympathies of men, and indulge in arbitrary and capricious habits of expression, in order to furnish food for fickle tastes, and fickle appetites, of their own creation. (287)

Wordsworth appears to be saying that he is writing for an audience, not just for himself, and that he expects to stir up the memories of his readers more effectively through the experience and language of everyday life. Being able to understand and to feel with him, they will be able to create meaning for themselves as they read the poems by adding to and re-creating what they already know.

A second important point Wordsworth makes is that he can never exactly replicate the language of real life and that the reader will never exactly read as the poet expected. Re-creation goes on in the acts of both writing and reading, and it is based on the individual memory storehouses of each particular reader and writer.

Finally, Wordsworth says that his poems usually have a purpose. This fact results from his "habits of meditation," which form his feelings:

> For all good poetry is the spontaneous overflow of powerful feelings: but though this be true, poems to which any value can be attached, were never produced on any variety of subjects but by a man, who being possessed of more than usual organic sensibility, had also thought long and deeply. For our continued influxes of feeling are modified and directed by our thoughts, which are indeed the representatives of all our past feelings; and, as by contemplating the relation of these general representatives to each other we discover what is really important to men, so, by the repetition and continuance of this act, our feelings will be connected with important subjects. (287)

Thinking, remembering, associating, and then re-creating are the acts that make poetry valuable. All are acts that rely on, in fact spring from, an active memory.

Here, therefore, in the Romantic literary tradition, we can find memory treated as a driving force in the composing process. It is a source of creation and a precursor to invention. But this tradition was far removed from the rhetorical studies of the times. And the enormous differences between rhetoric and romantic literature in the 18th and 19th century did not just separate the two fields for a short while. The separation appears to have turned into a complete divorce. In practice, most literary and rhetorical studies today take place in different spheres.

Many scholars today argue that the two fields need to be brought back together. James Berlin, for instance, insists that the empowering classroom is necessarily interdisciplinary ("Rhetoric" 491). Jay L. Robinson states that "privileged definitions" of literature, reading and writing do not fit the college clientele or the intellectual world today (251); however, the fields must join together not by "shotgun marriage" (252) but by building new theories that "reshape our departments and alter their priorities" (247). The theory that underlies this book—that memory is an active, constructive force important to the generation of ideas, knowledge, and writing—seems an appropriate theory to help join these and other fields of thought, scholarship, and teaching together.

* * *

As we examine memory's importance as a canon of rhetoric, we cannot look to the last 150 years of rhetorical theory for evidence of memory's value. The teaching of writing has concentrated primarily on concerns of style and arrangement. *Rhetoric* has been a term used only when essays are deemed "persuasive"; otherwise the term has been relegated to speech departments. However, I hope I've shown that right within the traditional rhetoric texts of the past we can find solid ground for memory to rest upon. There is plenty of evidence that memory has long been viewed as a precursor to invention and the other rhetorical canons, and that without memory, there is simply nothing to say.

The following chapters build a more complete theory of memory to guide us as we try to help students write. Building such a theory demands that we move outside English studies. The next three chapters show how scholars in philosophy, psychology, and literary studies have viewed memory and how they have given it a place in the making and conveyance of knowledge. Perhaps these chapters will help readers to structure their own "memory theaters," places filled with evidence of the value of memory to writers and teachers of writing.

A chapter that received its inspiration from the work of Francis Yates should end with her words. She expresses so well the enticement of studying memory:

> The art of memory is a clear case of a marginal subject, not recognised as belonging to any of the normal disciplines, having been omitted because it was no one's business. And yet it has turned out to be, in a sense, everyone's business. The history of the organisation of memory touches at vital points on the history of religion and ethics, of philosophy and psychology, of art and literature, of scientific method. The artificial memory as a part of rhetoric belongs into the rhetoric tradition; memory as a power of the soul belongs with theology. When we reflect on these profound affiliations of our theme it begins to seem after all not so surprising that the pursuit of it should have opened up new views of some of the greatest manifestations of our culture. (*Art* 389)

Chapter 3

Memory and Psychology

Musings

I prepared for the morning's appointments: I donned my white coat, stacked my files, and straightened the cushions on the couch. A knock on my door. I turned around to find Susan Bridges in the doorway.

"Hi, Susan! Come on in."

Susan is short and plump with great teeth and a cap of naturally curly black hair. She laid her books on the extra chair, tossed her ski jacket on top of them, and stretched out on my couch.

"Now close your eyes and relax," I told her in a soothing voice. I sat poised on the edge of my chair, clipboard and pencil in hand. "Tell me, Susan, what would you like to talk about today?"

"Third grade," she said quickly. "I've got to deal with third grade. Third grade was the year I kept getting Fs on penmanship quizzes. That's when I first knew I was a bad writer."

With furrowed brow, I scribbled quick notes on the clipboard. I leaned over, just enough to touch her gently, reassuringly on the head.

"Don't worry, Susan," I said in my most confident and reassuring voice, "We can take care of all that."

I made that scene up. It's fiction. Nothing like that happened at all.

What really happened is that I asked my writing students to answer a couple of questions about memory and writing. One of the questions was "What do you remember about writing in the past? Consider childhood, any writing you did on your own, teachers, advice you got—anything." I didn't know what I'd get or if it would be interesting or useful.

I imagined all sorts of brain activity going on as my students walked through the memory theaters of their minds. I imagined doors opening at every turn, bringing into view another piece of a past called "My Writing History." I imagined them writing furiously about this moment, then another, then another. And most of them did write furiously. But when I read over their papers, I realized that, for most of them, only one door opened, and what lay within was either an angel or a devil. I decided that the answers were more fitting for a psychologist than a writing teacher to cope with.

One of the girls really was the Susan Bridges I wrote about here. Her enthusiasm about writing ended with third-grade penmanship.

Tina told me this: "I used to write short stories all the time and was told that my short stories had some excellent ideas and imagination. Then I wrote my 10th-grade teacher a seven-page short story and she flunked me. She said that my story was by far the best in the class but she gave me an F because of my spelling and punctuation. Since then I haven't written a short story."

Michelle wrote, "My English teacher in high school was wonderful and it's because of her that I learned to put my feelings down on paper. I guess that's why I write best when I feel very strongly about something."

"Dread, pure and simple," were the first words on Mark's paper. "And because I hated writing in school so much, I never put any effort into personal writing either."

"This may sound ridiculous but my best memory about writing occurred in third grade. Each student in my class wrote a letter to an unknown pen pal and once we had them written, our teacher took us to a park and we put each letter inside of a helium-filled balloon and sent them off. There were at least 100 balloons in the sky. Surprisingly, some of us heard back from the people who found our balloons. I was one of the lucky ones." That was Gayle.

Sean said, "I always hated writing. I always hated when we were given a picture of something stupid and asked to write a short story about it. I mean what was that supposed to tell about us? The test happened every other year. A new story to go with a new picture."

This is from Michael: "My past was tough at first. My writings seemed to always be questioned and marked in red. Either the topic wasn't strong enough or my grammar or vocabulary seemed to be out of place or contained the wrong words that best suited the subject."

"In middle school it became important to write with better form—the Five-Paragraph essay. I hated squeezing my ideas into this form, but I was good at it. My papers were constantly the ones the teachers read in front of the class and I received a lot of resentment from other students. This is when I ceased to enjoy sharing my work," Julie wrote.

Ken told me, "It was always a tedious chore. In school I always had an assigned paper to write. It never was a choice that was left up to me. My teachers would pick the subject and then I would have to write on it, at the same time putting these words into exactly what they wanted to hear. My opinion had absolutely no meaning."

"I was the only left-hander in my sixth-grade class. When writing, I'd practically turn my paper all the way around until the teacher would turn it back (slanted to the left like a right-hander). This was an ongoing battle. All my papers were B papers because I didn't slant correctly. One day—it took me quite a while—I slanted to the right. She gave me an A." Stephanie wrote that.

Brian wrote this: "The most exciting time in my writing history was when I was in third grade and there was a young writer's award for the best story from each grade in our school. I worked really hard on my story, getting help from my mother, father, sister, and teacher. It was a cute story about a cookie. To make a long story short, I won the award for my class. I was really happy and I guess that's about the highlight of my writing history. After that most of my English teachers stressed proper English such as usage and punctuation so it wasn't that much fun."

I remember Michael Holzman's advice to writing teachers: "Try not to do any harm if you can help it." It's much like a line I came across the other day in a book by a psychologist and memory specialist, Elizabeth Loftus (Eyewitness 47). She says:

> *People's memories are fragile things. It is important to realize how easily information can be introduced into memory, to understand why this happens, and to avoid it when it is undesirable.*

All of a sudden being a writing teacher seems like a much scarier job.

* * *

Memory is clearly the enabling capacity of human existence. Without memory's capacity to store information in the remarkable quantities we generally take for granted, human behavior, human consciousness, and human identity would bear no relation to their present form. Without memory we couldn't engage in even the simplest and most familiar behaviors—tying our shoes, writing our names, or giving our telephone numbers—not to mention much more complex behaviors, such as preparing our meals, driving our cars, or filing our taxes. Consciousness without reminiscing or ruminating, awareness without last week's knowledge, and thinking without the information of a life history are hard to imagine. ... We might argue that none of these human achievements would actually be possible without memory. In short, memory allows us to be fully human. (Goethals and Solomon 1)

I am not a student of psychology. I began my search into psychological theories of memory knowing very little and remembering even less from the college psychology classes of my past. But I wanted to find out as much as possible about the ways psychologists study memory and the conclusions to which they've come, for their findings would certainly bring to light information about the making of knowledge that would connect to the process of writing. This chapter is the result of that search.

What follows is an overview of psychologists' efforts to understand memory. What psychologists have learned about memory proves that memory helps to create what we know and therefore is critical to concepts of knowledge and the rhetoric which communicates it. From psychologists we can learn how memory stores, retrieves, and creates knowledge.

The amount of information on memory in the discipline of psychology is staggering. A text in cognitive psychology might easily devote over half its pages to memory: For instance, the first 250 pages of John Anderson's 450-page *Cognitive Psychology and Its Implications* explain how the memory system works. But cognitive psychology is not the only branch of the discipline that can inform us about memory; other branches of psychology do so as well. Psychoanalysts have studied memory since the time of Freud, seeking to understand the unconscious processes of the mind. Freud believed that the unconscious held repressed memories that could only be retrieved with great effort. Social psychologists examine both how the culture affects our individual memories and how the culture itself may have a memory of its own. Studying memory as a social phenomenon provides valuable insights into the attitudes, stereotypes, and prejudices of cultures. And today the most exciting new discoveries about memory come from neuroscientific research—discoveries which suggest that memory is made up of complicated processes occurring in many domains of the brain. (For a good, comprehensive collection of the influential works on memory, see the three-volume *The Psychology of Memory*, edited by Peter E. Morris and Martin A. Conway.)

One way of looking at the way memory works within the mind is the psychoanalytic theory of Sigmund Freud. In works written throughout his life, some of which date back almost 100 years, Freud has described the workings of the mind by dividing it into the conscious, the preconscious, and the unconscious. The conscious, obviously, contains information of which we are at the moment aware. The preconscious contains information that we know but have not been thinking about, information that we are aware of having stored away. It is from the preconscious that we readily bring information to consciousness. The unconscious, however, contains material that is latent or has been repressed, often in early childhood. It is this material that surprises us when it is retrieved—when it comes to consciousness unexpectedly or when it appears in dreams.

It seems clear that both the preconscious and the unconscious involve the workings of long-term memory. Long-term memory can provide us with information we once knew, then stored away and now need again. But it also holds a great deal of experience that we do not realize we have stored, which has either been repressed or latent, or, like physical or artistic abilities, will never be part of our conscious mind.

Freud's theory points out the elusiveness of memory. In many ways, memory is unreliable: It can be stubborn, eccentric, and unpredictable. Information is received in, retained in, reconstructed in, and retrieved from memory in different ways: The individual memory that comes out is "a highly personal mental artifact" (Jeremy Campbell 228). Martin Conway and David Rubin call memories "compilations, constructions, or compositions of knowledge" (104); they are "temporary structures constructed and briefly retained in working memory" (128). Memories are changeable and ephemeral.

This unreliability can be both good and bad for writers, so it is important that we be aware of it. For instance, as teachers we can make our students aware of the ways their memories work, can help them when they need to bring back a memory suitable to the present "culture" (the memory of the form for MLA format, for instance), and can allow them to take advantage of the differences in memory that may turn their writing into delightful discourse. For it is differences in memory that allow us to write as individuals rather than as culturally programmed robots. In the same way that Richard Rorty values abnormal discourse, psychologist Frederick Bartlett, writing in 1932, saw value in the unique memory:

> Memory cannot be entirely extinguished in man, his capacity for experience cannot be entirely suppressed by schematization. It is in those experiences which transcend the cultural schemata, in those memories of experience which transcend the conventional memory schemata, that every new insight and every true work of art have their origin, and that the hope of progress, of a widening of the scope of human endeavor and human life, is founded. (26)

In addition, encouraging expression that takes advantage of the individual memory—which is always built on a unique combination of cultural memories—can help us to encourage alternative rhetorics and the study of the *memoria* that create them. This idea is pursued at the end of this chapter and developed fully in the last chapter.

Recent Developments in Memory Studies

Psychologists have actively studied memory throughout the 20th century. Most research in the past was done on impaired or exceptional memories. (Compare this to psychiatry's emphasis, which, until recently, focused on mental illness instead of mental health.) Although the findings of this research gave interesting and useful insights into the unusual memory case, many psychologists in the 1970s began to question whether the discipline was making enough advances in understanding how the natural, typical, unimpaired memory works. The concern was expressed by psychologists Tulving and Madigan in 1970:

> Many inventions and discoveries in other fields of human endeavor would bewilder and baffle Aristotle, but the most spectacular or counterintuitive finding from psychological studies of memory would cause him to raise his eyebrows only for an instant. At the time when man has walked on the moon, is busily transplanting vital organs from one living body into another, and has acquired the power to blow himself off the face of the earth by the push of a button, he still thinks about his own memory processes in terms readily translatable into ancient Greek. (qtd. in Kail 181)

Ulric Neisser expressed similar doubts in 1978: "We have an intellectually impressive group of theories, but history offers little confidence that they will provide any meaningful insight into natural behavior" (qtd. in Kail 181). However, writing 11 years later, Neisser cites the last 20 years as a time of great strides for memory research. These advances have occurred on two fronts. The first is the discovery by neuroscientists about how memory works in the brain. Particularly important is the belief now that there are different domains of memory in the brain for different memory tasks—semantic, autobiographical, spatial, skills, etc. (Neisser, "Domains" 68). If Aristotle would have only raised his eyebrows at the lack of progress before this time, he might be amazed at the advances of the next two decades; progress in science has taken students of memory into whole new areas of research. The exciting fact about this research is that it begins to make clear that memory is crucial to the generation of ideas and knowledge, that what we know depends on the workings of our memory.

The second major advance is the shift among many cognitive psychologists from studying memory through controlled laboratory experiments to studying the natural, everyday uses of memory in the environment. Neisser is a forerunner of this effort; he believes that psychologists should study how memory really works under real life conditions, how memory of the past is put to use in the present and the future (Neisser, *Memory* 12). As Robert Kail says, "Experimental psychologists have been admonished to leave the clear waters of verbal learning to probe the murky depths of ecological memory" (81).

Like researchers in rhetoric and composition studies, psychologists are beginning to see the advantages of natural study (Flower and Hayes are a particularly appropriate example; their work is discussed in chapter 6). The switch to a naturalistic mode of studying memory is attributed to American psychologist James Jenkins. He believes it is important to study memory "top down" (Jeremy Campbell 221)—to start with a person's experience of what is to be remembered. This is a behavior→brain approach, rather than the brain→behavior approach of most cognitive laboratory experiments. Its emphasis is on observing and describing rather than theorizing. It is very much the opposite of what had taken place in psychology; for example, "learning theory," under which much of the memory study in the last 30 years was done, had been almost exclusively brain→behavior, experimentally oriented. The addition of naturalistic study to research methods has made it easier to look at the memories of individuals and to study them as unique centers for the storage, retrieval, and creation of knowledge. Studying memory naturalistically leads to examining the individual and cultural influences on each person's memory, a practice that helps us understand better the creative processes of thinking and composing.

An important part of memory study, which began with Frederick Bartlett in 1932 but has been central in the last 20 years, is the view of memory as a reconstructive rather than a reproductive process. This view questions the fidelity to the original of that which is retrieved from the memory. As Jenkins says, "I think we will eventually conclude that the mind remembers what the mind does, not what the world does" (Jenkins 170; qtd. in Campbell 228). What the mind actually does is the subject of much psychological research, and the reconstruction process of memory is an exciting and elusive investigative subject. David Rubin, author of *Autobiographical Memory*, believes that research shows us that "memory creates

as well as distorts" (4) and that we need to figure out how it does so. This view
contradicts the classical view of the memory as a replicator of images and
experiences, but it opens the door to a definition which acknowledges that experiences in our culture cause us to reconstruct our view of the past.

Obviously the study of memory today covers diverse territory, from the sophisticated laboratories of neurochemists to the natural environments of everyday
people using their memories for everyday chores. The results of a national interdisciplinary conference on memory in 1988, recorded by Solomon, Goethals,
Kelley, and Stephens in *Memory: Interdisciplinary Approaches*, and in 1991, in
Theories of Memory edited by Collins, Gathercole, Conway, and Morris, show that
the goals and issues may not even be the same for different kinds of research into
memory.

The task that seems most interesting to those who study memory is that of
creating a model of memory, trying to understand how knowledge is represented
in memory. And it seems that our best prospect for truly understanding how memory
works lies in an interdisciplinary approach—combining cognitive and social
psychology, neuroscience, philosophy, and even the humanities. Psychologist
David Rubin says in *Autobiographical Memory* that the humanities can add to what
psychology knows: "Considering the literary autobiographies and histories themselves as complex human behaviors enriches our data base" (8). This statement
exemplifies the fact that, in yet another way, psychologists are looking at natural,
typical examples of how memory works, and, rather than only generalizing about
memory, are making clear that it is an idiosyncratic phenomenon, susceptible to a
plethora of influences.

A Cognitive Model of Human Memory

Most psychologists view memory in three components: In cognitive terms, these
are the sensory memory, the short-term memory, and the long-term memory.

The sensory memory (sensory register, sensory store) allows us to become aware
of information; that information may be held there for a few seconds. Most
psychologists believe that there is a different sensory memory for each sense; that
is, auditory experiences are stored and processed differently, in a different brain
area, than visual experiences.

The pattern recognition box in Fig. 3.1 is much like a filter. We compare new
information with what we know. A typical psychology text example is to show
A 13 C and 12 13 14 —our interpretation of the middle figure depends on the
context provided by the outer two. We recognize, reconstruct, and interpret depending on that context (Benjamin, Hopkins, and Nation 236). Obviously, our attention
and our memory are selective. We could never attend or process every stimulus
around us. This selection process occurs not only with what we notice, but with
what we take unnoticed into short-term memory as well.

Our short-term memory holds only a few items of information and only for a
short time. Unless information is *rehearsed*—unless we repeat it to ourselves

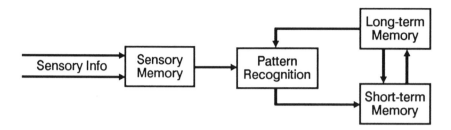

FIG. 3.1. Information-processing model of human memory.

mentally—it will be lost within seconds. Short-term memory keeps information in an active state either before it is sent to or when it is retrieved from long-term memory. We are using short-term memory, for example, when we try to remember a phone number long enough to get from the phone book to the phone. Seven digits are not too tough for most of us, if we rehearse along the way, but evidently eight numbers is much more difficult.

Some information is lost from short-term memory, but that which we keep goes to long-term memory. No one knows how much of what we sense and attend actually gets into our long-term memory, but the space in long-term memory appears to be limitless. We cannot overload it. Elizabeth Loftus estimates that we can store one quadrillion bits of separate information in long-term memory (*Memory* 15). It is not getting information into long-term memory that is difficult; rather, it is retrieving it.

The model of memory developed by cognitive psychologists has been the basis for some of the important research done in composition, particularly the work of Linda Flower and John Hayes. Flower and Hayes include the long-term memory as one of the three elements in the writing process. It is important for storing not only personal memories but strategies for writing as well. Using a cognitive model, Flower and Hayes explain how writers work back and forth between long-term and short-term memory: retrieving possibilities from long-term, assessing and reconstructing them in short-term, going back to long-term for more possibilities, and so on, until a piece of writing is produced. Their work is discussed further in chapter 6.

Short-term memory was the concern of ancient orators who memorized their speeches: How could they best remember their speeches long enough to deliver them? Long-term memory involves the retrieval of information that is not purposely memorized or readily retrievable, and modern memory studies focus more on long-term memory. In his important article, "The Art of Memory Reconceived: From Rhetoric to Psychoanalysis," Patrick Hutton expresses the change of focus differently: "The image of memory as a brightly-lit theater of the world was replaced by ... memory as a mirror of the dark abyss of the mind" (130). It is that dark abyss, the long-term memory, that is interesting for the purposes of this study: what is in there; how it is stored, transmuted, and retrieved; and what value it has for the present and the future. The various facets of long-term memory are discussed in the next few pages: the way information is stored in memory, the concepts of schemata and metamemory, and the consideration of memory as reconstruction rather than replication of the past. That is followed by a discussion of the inaccuracies of memory, of forgetting, of the practicality of memory, and of unexpected or unbidden memories. By approaching the enigma of long-term memory from these various angles, we begin to see what kind of a body of knowledge both we and our students have at our disposal when we think, when we act, and when we write.

How Memories are Stored

Neuroscience is a new field in the study of memory. In recent years, neuroscientists and cognitive scientists have joined ranks and together have come up with new and exciting information about the workings of memory.

Psychologists assumed for a long time that memory, that "dark abyss of the mind," occupied a certain place in the brain. Much of their searching has been to find that place in the mind where memory lurks. Neuroscientific research, however, shows that memory is not a localized spot in the brain, but that different sites throughout the brain store or register different types of memories. "Human memory is not a broad power, but comprises numerous separate abilities. Each is carried out in a specific place in the brain" (Hilts C8). Different neural systems, perhaps parallel circuits, mediate what we know, and there are cellular changes in the brain which occur because of experience (McGaugh 37). McGaugh states that "Memory is, of course, not a 'thing': Rather, memory is an outcome of the functioning of a complex set of neurobiological processes" (34).

Interestingly, this is similar to established models of cognition as parallel distributed processes (PDP), in which different parts of the brain switch on and react to each other at the same time. The PDP line of thinking comes from the world of artificial intelligence; much cognitive work on learning and memory has been based on the computer as a model (Benjamin, Hopkins, and Nation 227). At the same time, computer architecture has been quite anthropomorphic, with processing power working first through random access (short-term) memory and then to storage (long-term) memory on hard disk.

The integrating part of the brain appears to be the hippocampus. Recent research by Zola-Morgan and Squire indicates that the hippocampus initially stores information before it is sent to different areas of the brain, and that it also consolidates memories for retrieval (289). Amnesia is caused by damage to the hippocampus. Yet the thalamus, the amygdala, parts of the prefrontal cortex, and the cerebellum itself have all been found to play a part in memory storage; there is growing consensus that different kinds of memory—declarative (learning what), procedural (learning how), semantic (general knowledge), and episodic (autobiographical knowledge)—are treated differently in the brain. The brain's own categories, Richard Thompson suggests, may be different than those of psychologists (18).

Owen Flanagan describes the needed change in our view of memory this way: Whereas the typical view of memory is that of a mental office manager or secretary filing and retrieving information, the new view may be of "a multifarious force of low-level specialists" or "army of idiots," which makes the mind "more like a committee than a unified whole" (176).

At the same time that this study of the structure of memory in the brain is going on, neurochemists are studying the chemical systems of the body to try to better understand memory and thought itself. Exciting new research is being done, for example, on a molecule called the NMDA receptor, which controls communication between brain cells. When it does not work, the network that creates memories fails. So far, scientists have been able to block the receptors in animals, preventing learning and memory (Benjamin, Hopkins, and Nation 262–263). Further investigation like this offers exciting possibilities to add to the traditional bodies and methods of memory research. The assumption is that learning and memory can be understandable through molecular analysis, a new field to add to those already involved in trying to solve the puzzle that is the human memory.

Memory researcher Larry Squire believes that the middle ground where neuroscience and psychology meet offers the greatest possibilities for truly understanding how memory works (1618). Complete understanding is still very far away: Despite all the advances in the sciences that probe it, memory remains very elusive. Says Howard Gardner, reviewing a book about the study of memory:

> while memory researchers might soon reach agreement about activities at the synaptic level, there are almost as many theories of memory in the large as there are rooms in that palatial structure. And an explanation of the phenomena of memory that most intrigue us—from Slavic bards who can recite 30,000 verses by heart to the floodgates opened by Proust's taste of a pastry—remain remote from the best scientific minds and the best science writers of our time. ("Mind Explorers")

Metamemory, Schemata, and Reconstruction

"Metamemory" is the term used for awareness of or knowledge about memory, its value, and how it works. Although most study on metamemory is developmental, and therefore done with children, it appears that adults have a highly developed metamemorial sense. What we construct are personal models of memory: "the set of articulable beliefs ... about the general nature of human memory and [our] own particular capabilities" (Klatzky 109). These models are often based on folk wisdom, according to Roberta Klatzky. Some of this wisdom is quite accurate—that we retain all we get through the senses, that differences come in the retrieval process; that altering the mind can both help and block retrieval. But some parts of the folk wisdom are myth rather than scientific truth—belief in hypnosis as a memory aid, belief in photographic memory, and common understanding of amnesia and of memory loss due to aging (124–130). But despite these myths and despite the difficulty in assessing what one really knows about memory, research shows that people generally seem to have a reasonable and stable metamemorial sense.

Today psychologists and neuroscientists think that information is stored in long-term memory in an abstract form. We think we remember visually and in words, but that is just because we convert retrieved items to pictures and words so quickly upon recall. According to John Anderson, the theory that memories are stored abstractly is the great accomplishment of modern cognitive psychology (123). This theory is upheld by the fact that we remember meaning much longer than we remember physical details. Psychologists generally agree that we put items into long-term memory by associating them with items already in there, by creating and recognizing relationships. Context and association are important parts of retention in and retrieval from long-term memory. Basically, we remember best that which is meaningful to our lives. These ideas are similar to those of reading theorist Frank Smith, who defines what we know—what is in our memories—as our "theory of what the world is like" (*Understanding* 7). (Further connections with Smith are made in chapter 6.)

These associations and relationships are made easily because of *schemata*—the organizational structures we make in our mind as we correlate and categorize experience to create, defend, and modify our world views. Anderson defines schemata as "large, complex units of knowledge that organize much of what we know about general categories of objects, classes of events, and types of people" (128). Schemata that cause us to expect certain sequences of action are called *scripts*; those which cause us to label individuals or groups are *stereotypes*. And although schemata are powerful, essential means of processing and retaining information, they are subject to bias and distortion (129). For instance, Frederick Bartlett did an experiment telling people a story called "The War of the Ghosts" from a traditional Indian society. When the people retold the story, they systematically changed it to fit with their own cultural ideas of story schemata (Anderson 153; Bartlett 118–124). All references to ghosts were filtered out of the retold stories, reflecting the fact that the White culture of the study's subjects does not believe in ghosts. Craig Barclay, in "Schematization of Autobiographical Memory," looks at literary autobiography as a way to study memory processes. What he finds is that autobiography may be inaccurate in detail, but that it must keep the integrity of the life (86): "what is remembered is compatible with one's existing self-knowledge" (88). Ernest Schachtel, writing in 1947, argued that the phenomenon of infantile amnesia—the inability to remember our first years of life—is not due to the repression of infant sexuality, as Freud had postulated. Instead, he says, childhood amnesia is based on the fact that we have no use for those experiences in our adult schemata (4). (His is not the only alternative theory to Freud's—Katherine Nelson suggests, for instance, that language is what allows us autobiographical memory, and we cannot remember the early years because we did not have language (148).)

It was 50 years ago that Frederick Bartlett wrote his book on memory, but his explanation of the importance of schemata still stands today:

Remembering is not the re-excitation of innumerable fixed, lifeless and fragmentary traces. It is an imaginative reconstruction, built out of the relation of our attitude towards a whole active mass of organized past reactions or experiences, and to a little outstanding detail which commonly appears in image or in language form. It is thus hardly ever really exact ... and it is not at all important that it should be so. The attitude is literally an effect of the organism's capacity to turn round upon its own "schemata" and is directly a function of consciousness. (213)

Memory is a reconstructive process, and the reconstruction depends a great deal on the schemata that define and organize our lives.

Once we acknowledge that memory is primarily reconstructive rather than replicative, we can begin to understand the complexities of coming up with any encompassing rules for how memory works. As Jeremy Campbell says, "What memory is depends on context, and contexts change" (222). Psychologists dating from William James have agreed that memory involves all the higher functions: We use perception, comprehension, inference, belief, and language, but in remembering we attribute all these functions to the past. How much and what we remember depends on the quality of the experience, and that differs for everybody (Jeremy Campbell 222). As Schachtel puts it, "Memory as a function of the living personality can be understood only as a capacity for the organization and reconstruction of past experiences and impressions in the service of present needs, fears, and interests (3). Remembering our past keeps us from repeating it; it is the basis for our self-improvement" (Loftus, *Memory* 121).

And research shows clearly that what occurs between the time an event occurs and the time it is retrieved can make a great deal of difference in how we remember. New experience alters both our previous experience and our behavior. Writer Dorothy Richardson, who pioneered the stream-of-consciousness method of writing in literature, believes that we reconstruct the past to make it compatible with our present world: "the past *and its meaning* are being continually remade in the interests of maintaining inner coherence" (Wallace and Gruber 163). Every time later information is added to what we know, it meshes together in memory. All of this is affected in many ways—by ways of thinking, by labels, by guessing, by stating something aloud (Loftus, *Eyewitness*).

When we retrieve a memory, then, it is probably based on certain real and important details. The rest have been forgotten, and, to fill in, we construct appropriate details to complete the picture.

As healthy persons, we constantly reconstruct what we know or remember to better fit the patterns we apply to the world in order to understand it. Remembering thus includes adding things, forgetting things, or putting them away into some suspended storage (Kelly 472). Bannister and Mair describe the theory of personal constructs this way:

If a man of twenty is asked to describe what his life was like when he was eight years old and is asked the same question at the age of fifty, the two accounts may not tally. The discrepancy does not have to be explained in terms of "loss" and "distortion." It can be argued that in the intervening years his personal construct system has altered and his view of what is important and unimportant, and what is signified by events, and what events are causally related, may all have changed. ... From a construct theory point of view, *remembering* and *understanding* are inextricably related. (214–215)

Are our memories then completely unreliable? Perhaps not completely, but certainly we cannot count on them for accurate replication of the past. Studies on eyewitness testimony best illustrate the unreliability of memory, as the work of Elizabeth Loftus shows. Neither truth serums or hypnosis necessarily result in true accounts of the past; they may just make the witness more relaxed and willing to talk. Even studies on brain stimulation that seem to show that stimulation around the hippocampus increases memory are suspect—is the brain remembering or making new experience?

Many variables, both inside and outside of our own heads, can change the way we remember. For example, Loftus found that when witnesses saw a videotape of a car accident and were asked about the speeds at which the cars were travelling, their estimates were much higher speeds if they were asked "How fast were the cars going when they smashed into each other?" than if they were asked how fast they were going when they "hit" each other (*Eyewitness* 115). Also, intervening events can affect and alter remembering a great deal. It is tempting to imagine a piece of information taken in, then lying dormant until retrieved. But Loftus emphasizes that much can happen to change how people think about or remember something during the time that the information is retained (*Eyewitness* 21).

Loftus concludes that "A healthy distrust of one's memory in general is not a bad idea. When all is said and done, memory is selective; the memory machine is selective about what gets in and selective about how it changes over time. This may be adaptive in many ways" (*Memory* 147). She sees this adaptive quality as a self-serving bias—we tend to see ourselves and what we have done in a better light (135).

In contrast, Ulric Neisser would be apt to agree with Barclay's conclusion about autobiographical memory—that although the past may be presented inaccurately in a technical, literal sense, the integrity of the life is maintained. In his case study of the Watergate testimony of John Dean, Neisser concludes that although Dean's testimony was inaccurate regarding specific incidents, "Dean was right about what really had been going on in the White House" (qtd. in Neisser, *Memory* 159). In other words, his testimony represented a generally accurate picture of the events in a larger perspective, in terms of some "What the White House Has Been Doing These Days" schema.

Forgetting

"I don't remember." Although we've heard this phrase frequently in political scandals like Watergate and Whitewater and have translated it as "I don't want to remember," all of us know that honest forgetting is a much-too-frequent occurrence in our daily lives. What, how much, and why do we forget? These are questions without clear answers. Most cognitive scientists believe that forgetting is not necessarily a loss of information but a loss of the ability to retrieve it (Anderson 180). The ability to remember is enhanced by repetition and rehearsal and, conversely, is hindered by lack of both as well as by interference from intervening or previous information. In fact, interference may be the biggest cause of forgetting. Forgetting occurs over time: Herman Ebbinghaus' first memory experiment in 1885, where he memorized a series of nonsense syllables himself, showed that although we remember more shortly after an event, the rate at which we forget is rather rapid at first, and then forgetting occurs at a much slower rate.

Some psychologists once believed that we forget because our memories decay with time. Most now believe that we forget because of interference that blocks the retrieval of a certain piece of information. For instance, I may not be able to remember lines from *Hamlet* right after reading *Macbeth*. The interference, *Macbeth*, comes between my learning and my retrieval attempt. If I look up a phone number and my daughter asks me a question before I reach the phone, I will probably have to look up the number again. Interference can block learning that comes *after* it, too. After my son was bitten by a German shepherd, I had trouble learning that my neighbor had a new shepherd with a good disposition. The new knowledge contradicted my existing experience.

Just as there are different kinds of memory, there are also different kinds of forgetting. In general, it is more common for a person to forget to do a future action than to forget having done a past one; the exception to this is forgetting when we hide something in a special place (Benjamin, Hopkins, and Nation 255). Forgetting in old age takes different forms. The elderly are more likely to forget something recent than something in the distant past, perhaps because their brains do not organize the new information as well as they did the old. And they do not forget how to do something they once knew how to do. Extreme forms of forgetting include retrograde amnesia, which is the forgetting of the past before the event which caused the amnesia, and anterograde amnesia, which is the inability to form memories after such an event (Benjamin, Hopkins, and Nation 256–259).

Experiments on the TOT phenomenon (tip-of-tongue) show that we use different strategies to try to remember a forgotten word, one that is on "the tip of the tongue." We know the information is somewhere in our memory, and we try to access it by making associations. The process is not haphazard. Not surprisingly, the words and names forgotten that allow us the greatest number of paths for retrieval are those likely to be retrieved. Through perseveration, we can often overcome a TOT block and pop up with the word or name minutes or hours later, when a new path, often unbidden and instantaneous, opens up.

Stress appears to have a strong influence on forgetting. It is associated with some types of amnesia as well as with small-time forgetting. And sometimes forgetting is driven by the desire to eliminate pain (Loftus, *Memory* 82). These facts fit with our first knowledge of forgetting, for according to Hesiod's *Theogyny*, Lethe (Forgetting) was the daughter of Eris (Strife) (Schachtel 25). Looking at the issue of forgetting helps to broaden our view of how memory actually works. It becomes more apparent as we study memory that it is much more than a storehouse; it is an active, vibrant entity, responding to the stimuli of daily life.

The Practicality and Predictability
of Memory

The idea that we might forget on purpose to avoid stress or pain suggests that memory is an adaptive, practical phenomenon. Katherine Nelson suggests that "Remembering the past has value insofar as it serves action in the present or future. Thus what is remembered should be that that enables the individual to carry out activities, to predict, and to plan" (144). Ulric Neisser lists six ways in which we use the past: (a) to define ourselves and give us an identity; (b) for self-improvement; (c) for public purposes, as with testimony; (d) to learn from others' experience; (e) to keep track of what we have to do; and (f) for use as an intellectual activity (*Memory* 14–17). These are functions of memory in our everyday lives.

Practicality makes us omit unnecessary information from memory, perhaps to make it possible to retrieve what we do consider important. An interesting example of this phenomenon is an experiment done by Nickerson and Adams in which they had subjects both draw a penny and identify the correct penny from 15 drawings. Hardly anyone could do either task right. Nickerson and Adams concluded that the visual details are probably not stored in memory because they are not necessary to identify and use a penny—they have no practical use.

Our practical need to remember leads us to use all kinds of external memory aids as well as our minds. We all have heard ourselves or our colleagues say "If I don't write it down, I won't remember it," and we mark as an organized person the one who carries a planner. We have photographs, scrapbooks, and mementos of our past. My children do not want to hear about my wedding; they want to see the picture album. Neisser says that people generally trust external aids more than their own memories. They believe they are more reliable (*Memory* 337). We understand the potential shortcomings of memory and do what we must to enhance our ability to remember. We expand our memories by writing things down.

A 5-year study by psychologist Paul Johnson reinforces the theory that memory operates both practically and individually. Johnson studied the ways that specialist physicians come up with their diagnoses. "Enormous individual differences appear" in their strategies, and Johnson concludes:

> You can make a large mistake in thinking that content is represented in memory in the same way as is represented in text books. Information is stored in memory according to the way in which the individual person knows it is going to be used. It is stored according to the demands of the tasks with which he is familiar. (qtd. in Jeremy Campbell 221)

Practicality certainly seems to affect literal recall. Neisser, in his essay "Literacy and Memory," points out that verbatim memorization is usually saved for socially important texts, such as the Gettysburg Address—those which "are self-defining; no other sequence of words is that text" (*Memory* 300). We memorize these texts even if we don't understand them—"Gladly, the cross-eyed bear" was the favorite church hymn of a child I once knew, and "Jose, can you see" began the national anthem many times in elementary school. We are more likely to memorize texts if our culture values their exact words. George Stratton discusses the phenomenon of the "Shass Pollak," one of many Hebrew scholars who had learned the *Talmud* by heart, not just literally but visually—he memorized exactly where everything was on every page (311). However, the less the culture values verbatim recall, the less likely texts are to be memorized. A study of traditional Yugoslavian oral poets found that although there were many similarities in the poems as they were sung by different poets, the singers themselves did not even understand the notion of "word for word"—their frames of reference were formulas and themes (Lord 245).

Although much of the study of memory has dealt with purposeful retrieval of things learned or experienced in the past, much of our memory works involuntarily—we are reminded of something which comes to us unbidden. Proust's petite madeleine opened the floodgates of memory for him. Russian novelist Esther Salaman calls these memories "precious fragments": She says that they are always full of emotion and make us live in the past for that moment (63). Less is understood about these memories, but certainly the fact that they occur frequently and often serve as inspiration—as a muse—is documented by writers throughout time. Memories which come back unbidden are thought to be important somehow, held deep in long-term memory. Perhaps the Freudian slip is an unbidden memory— something we have triggered, but we don't know how. Psychologists cannot explain exactly why or how these memories are remembered and retrieved, but their existence and reappearance strengthen the assumption that we remember a great deal more than we think we do; retrieval, not storage, is the problem.

Information that has been integrated or elaborated is easier to recall. John Anderson explains how elaboration works. We elaborate a piece of information by connecting it to prior knowledge, by using imagination or inferences on it, and by connecting the information to our present context (217). Elaboration helps us to remember through redundancy; we increase the connections to other pieces of information in our brains. These connections or contextual elements establish more pathways to retrieve the information—more ways to get it back (218). Unbidden memories apparently come back when a pathway is opened. We can aid remembering when we create more possible pathways. Elaboration also helps to impose a structure on memory, giving a mental search some organization and thus making it more efficient (205). This is probably the reason that recognition tests are usually easier than tests of recall—there are more paths to search for the proper information (164). This fact also justifies prewriting and multiple drafts in writing as well as repetition and review in teaching.

Context affects remembering—people remember best in the same physical or emotional environment where they first acquired the information. For instance, I should be more successful taking a test over facts in the same room where I first learned the facts; I should best be able to remember last year's feelings of depression while in another depressed state. I should even be able to better remember something that happened while I was drunk if I am drunk again! These physical and mental cues become important parts of the memory from the very beginning (Benjamin, Hopkins, and Nation 252). Other contextual factors at retrieval time also affect the ability to remember, as studies with eyewitnesses show: People make more errors if asked particular questions than if they are allowed to choose what to say, and, if they are asked questions, accuracy changes depending on the wording of the questions and on who is doing the asking (Loftus, *Eyewitness*).

Studying the workings of memory is fascinating for its own sake. It becomes even more so when we relate it to the processes that occur in our students' minds when we ask them to write. It is apparent that many operations are at work and that what we call "inventing" or "composing" are complicated by all sorts of phenomena outside the confines of the syllabus or the assignment.

Social Psychology and Memory

On one hand, memory research shows us how individual each person's memory is. No two people will filter, sort, store, or retrieve information in exactly the same way. On the other hand, memory responds to the environment that we inhabit. We organize our memories by schemata which are meaningful to our lives. Memory is adaptive and functions to fit our present needs. In other words, memory has a social side as well—the contents and organization and product of our memories have a great deal to do with the world in which we live and the traditions of our culture. Students of social memory, a new field, address these issues. Social memory researchers study how people use what they comprehend and learn, how they make judgments and behavioral decisions (Wyer 243). These researchers examine the behavior and attitudes of people in a social context in order to understand how memory affects these attitudes and belief systems.

Social memory is akin to Carl Jung's "collective unconscious":

> In addition to our immediate consciousness, which is of a thoroughly personal nature and which we believe to be the only empirical psyche, ... there exists a second psychic system of a collective, universal, and impersonal nature which is identical in all individuals. This collective unconscious does not develop individually but is inherited. It consists of pre-existent forms, the archetypes, which can only become conscious secondarily and which give definite form to certain psychic contents. (*Archetypes* 43)

These archetypes are "primordial images" which symbolize the experience of being human. They are unconscious; Philipson suggests that the archetypes provide "the conditions for imaginative thought" (59). Jung says, "The fact is that archetypal images are so packed with meaning in themselves that people never think of asking what they really do mean" (*Archetypes* 13). In *Psychological Types*, he refers to the primordial image as "a mnemic deposit, an imprint" (qtd. in Philipson 58), like an individual memory trace waiting to be used.

Interestingly, today the most compelling and successful video games world-wide, whether from California or Japanese programmers, are based on some of these same archetypal themes and drives—for example, they involve battles against magical enemies and the salvation or rescue or theft by a male hero of a female heroine. And video games are a strong force in popular culture. Eugene Provenzo, in his book *Video Kids: Making Sense of Nintendo*, believes that video games "both reflect and shape our culture" (118). We might be wise to worry, for video games are often based on themes of aggression and violence that emphasize individual success and gender stereotypes, showing women as dependent and victimized (116). Reinforcing these themes in the minds of our children may have dangerous antisocial consequences:

> We cannot stand outside of the context and connections of culture and be fully realized as human beings. Video games, in their emphasis on violence and the self as an autonomous being, disregard this truth. (131–132)

The vivid response by players to these themes seems to be almost genetic, certainly crossing cultures. The archetypes may not be those we want to form the collective unconscious of our children's generation.

Jung defines the collective unconscious as part of the human genetic heritage, possessed by all people. Other psychologists have taken the idea of the collective unconscious and used it to explain differences in gender, race, and specific cultures. Sigmund Freud says, for instance, in *An Outline of Psychoanalysis*,

> I believe it is not impossible that we may be able to discriminate between that part of the latent mental processes which belong to the early days of the individual and that which has its roots in the infancy of the race. ... symbolism, a mode of expression which has never been individually acquired, may claim to be regarded as a racial heritage. (qtd. in Bennett 91)

Memory helps us root ourselves in something larger than our daily experience. Freud suggests that our memories are full of "ideational contents, memory traces of former generations" (from *Moses and Monotheism*, qtd. in Bennett 91). Patrick Hutton, in "The Art of Memory Reconceived," emphasizes that all attempts to develop memory systems are attempts to get back to the roots of a civilization. Bruno's magical memory theater, Vico's stages of civilization, and Freud's psycho-analysis are all structures "based on the premise that imagination is born of memory" (390–391). Each is based "upon the faith that humans have the capacity to recover all human experiences that have been forgotten and thereby to make the record of human history whole" (391).

Frederick Bartlett says that the collective unconscious in social psychology is like memory traces in the individual: "Both appear to assume that psychological material—images, symbols, ideas, formulae—are somehow individually preserved and stored up for use" in a person or "somewhere in a persistent psychical structure which is the possession of a social group" (281).

Bartlett refers to the work of Maurice Halbwachs, who studied the collective memory of families, religious groups, and social classes. These memories, Bartlett tells us, are

> no mere series of individualized images of the past ... they are also models, examples, a kind of basis for education and development. In them is expressed the general attitude of the group, so that they do more than reproduce its history, they define its nature, its strength and its weaknesses. (295)

Bartlett does not argue that there is a "group memory" which supersedes individual memory; in fact, he is not sure at all that there is such a thing as a collective unconscious. But Halbwachs' work demonstrates that the group is a memory-making body, one which helps determine the schemata that organize the individual brains of the group's members. Bartlett concludes:

> Whether the social group has a mental life over and above that of its individual members is a matter for speculation and belief. That the organised group functions in a unique and unitary manner in determining and directing the mental lives of its individual members is a matter of certainty and of fact. (300)

As a culture dies out, its memories are lost if they are not recorded. A *TIME* cover story bemoans the loss of knowledge of primitive tribes as technology takes over worldwide:

> Stored in the memories of elders, healers, midwives, farmers, fishermen and hunters in the estimated 15,000 cultures remaining on earth is an enormous trove of wisdom. ... the world's tribes are dying out or being absorbed into modern civilization. As they vanish, so does their irreplaceable knowledge. (Linden 46)

TIME reports that this is tragic for the tribes: "the soul of their culture withers away" (48). But the price of forgetting may be great for the rest of the world as well, especially in light of the "developed world's disastrous mismanagement of the environment":

> some scientists are beginning to recognize that the world is losing an enormous amount of basic research as indigenous peoples lose their culture and traditions. Scientists may someday be struggling to reconstruct this body of wisdom to secure the developed world's future. (48)

Exciting efforts are taking place to reinvent the Polynesian art of navigation, an art which allowed ancient Polynesians to travel thousands of miles at sea with no navigational instruments, using knowledge in their memories to guide them. The efforts to reinvent a lost cultural art have helped legitimize research in the field of "experimental archaeology" as its researchers try to recreate the vessels, knowledge, and conditions of the past in order to "remember" what their ancestors' culture knew (Finney; Hutchinson).

Group memory can be a negative force as well as a positive one, and life might be more pleasant for many if some group memories, or attitudes, were forgotten. When attitudes are held by a social group, they become stronger through the reinforcement of others. Not only are the attitudes held by the group thus strengthened, but, when the attitudes result in stereotyping another group, the attitudes of the stereotyped group are affected as well, according to social psychologist Eliot Aronson: "When we hold erroneous beliefs or stereotypes about other people, our responses to them often cause them to behave in ways that validate these erroneous beliefs" (243). Group memories thus permeate the lives of both the holders of the original view and the subjects of that view.

Some psychologists would argue that along with memories held by individuals in groups, there is indeed a collective memory. The attempt to pursue and define it is the study of the new field of social memory, which, according to Thomas Ostrom, "is still trying to define its major problems" (201). Ostrom credits the first real interest in collective memory to Maurice Halbwachs; he looks at Halbwachs' *La Memoire Collective*, written while he was in a German concentration camp during World War II. Ostrom summarizes Halbwachs' thesis: "all memory is collective ... memory cannot be understood without simultaneously understanding the milieu in which the person resides" (213). Ostrom thinks ideas like those of Halbwachs are a key to future study of social memory, and that they "are fully congruent with contemporary information-processing conceptions. ... Memory is socially distributed ... other people serve as satellite memory stores that the individual can access upon need" (213).

* * *

New memory research is burgeoning in psychology and the sciences. Recently, I opened my morning *Denver Post* and found the headline "Scientists hope to tap brain's fountain of youth" emblazoned atop a page. Following were three long articles detailing the amazing recent biochemical advances in understanding and influencing the memory. Memory is becoming less elusive, and the new knowledge is out there to be consumed by the general newspaper-reading public.

The more we are able to understand how memory deposits, retrieves, and reconstructs information, the more we will know how we can best use it to facilitate writing and teaching. We will more clearly comprehend how learning takes place.

We can learn even more by using the knowledge we glean from social psychologists. Gender, religious background, racial background and specific culture all affect the way we perceive and are perceived. So social memory can be a factor in memory study in two different ways. First, the cultural memories we each hold affect the way that we interpret and react to our world; they both help us to conform and keep us from conforming. Second, the way that we react to our world based on those cultural memories affects the way we are seen and accepted by others. As our own individual but socially constructed memories meet the memory of our culture—as we assess our own histories and traditions against those of our larger world—they combine, sometimes easily, sometimes not. The person that we create out of the chaos of all these memories is who we are.

Chapter 4

Memory and Philosophy

Musings

I am trying to remember the last name of my college friend Kathy. I have just met someone who grew up in her hometown. It's a fairly small town; they're the same age—surely they knew one another. I open the front door of my personal memory theater and find my past in orderly and complete fashion. My "theater" has an efficient floor plan, so I know I can get myself quickly to the "college days" room. And that room, like all the others, is spotless and organized, so without much trouble I'll find the shelf upon which I have arranged old friends, and before long I'll have her last name—a recollection of a segment of my past, ready to use again.

But this only happens in my imagination. In reality, my memory theater is more like a haunted house. It's Victorian, full of nooks and crannies and secret places. It's dark, dilapidated, and dusty, and it smells of mildew. I have to climb creaking stairs to get to many of the rooms. Some of their doors I'm afraid to open. Others just won't open: The past seems locked away from me, and I hear it chuckle from behind those doors. When I do open a door, I find the room within messy and unbearably full. Nothing is as it should be, and the furnishings of the room are now broken, stained, or missing. What I get for my trouble, for my efforts to remember, are a frustration headache and some bits and pieces of what I wanted—a fact here, a date there, a fleeting image and a tug on my heart. This is all I can recollect, and from it I re-create a moment gone by. Occasionally, if I talk about that moment with someone who might recall it too, she will say, "No, you've got it wrong; it wasn't like that at all."

Trying to write a coherent chapter on the role of memory in philosophy is much like trying to use my own memory. However, if my memory theater is a haunted house, philosophy's might be the Pentagon: it's huge, complex, and guarded. But I must go there, for the "philosophy" nook in my dark house is very dusty indeed. It gives me little. It holds back all it can and seems to taunt me. So I head to philosophy's Pentagon, only to find that I need special access to get in. This search is not for everybody. My access comes from my colleague, Sally the philosophy professor, who gives me books and names and suggestions, the clout I need to get into the long corridors of the building. All the halls look the same, and the small labels on them do not help me. No doors say "Memory and Philosophy"—the organization here is different than mine would be, and far more complex. My only hope, I can see, is to somehow get a master key, and sneak into rooms at night.

I manage to get the key. I prowl around after dark, wrongly starting at the inner of the five rings which make up the Pentagon floor plan. Only by luck and long hours do I find that important people are housed in the outer ring, the one with windows to the outside world. Here, finally, I begin to occasionally say "aha!" When I'm finished here, I have stacks of information to look through—thoughts, borrowed books, and recommendations for books from still other rooms, all part of the 2,000 years of texts and criticism of western philosophy. I feel like "S," Aleksandr Luria's mnemonist whose memory was always so full of information that he found it almost impossible to organize or ignore any of it. Like S, I will try to discriminate between what is useful and what is not. I will try to take from philosophy's Pentagon a few items to help me furnish one small but rich corner in my own house which I can then label "philosophy and memory." But all the time I am doing this, I will be uncomfortable. I will think of the three lower floors of that Pentagon, the floors that I could never get to with doors that my single master key could never open, and I will be humble.

* * *

The text started with the premise that if rhetoric is to be taught at all at a University level it should be taught as a branch of reason, not as a mystic art. Therefore it emphasized a mastery of the rational foundations of communication in order to understand rhetoric. Elementary logic was introduced, elementary stimulus–response theory was brought in, and from these a progression was made to an understanding of how to develop an essay.

For the first year of teaching Phaedrus had been fairly content with this framework. He felt there was something wrong with it, but that the wrongness was not in this application of reason to rhetoric. The wrongness was in the old ghost of his dreams—rationality itself. He recognized it as the same wrongness that had been troubling him for years, and for which he had no solutions. He just felt that no writer ever learned to write by this squarish, by-the-numbers, objective, methodical approach. Yet that was all rationality offered and there was nothing to do about it without being irrational. And if there was one thing he had a clear mandate to do in this Church of Reason it was to be rational, so he had to let it go at that. (Pirsig 176)

It is impossible to go through the history of memory without moving into philosophy's territory, partly because the same great thinkers addressed issues in both philosophy and rhetoric, and partly because the notion of memory is vital to a wide variety of disciplines, including philosophy.

"Memory" as such is not directly addressed that often in philosophy. What philosophers address more, along with man's nature and purpose, is how we know—theories of knowledge. In every era, philosophers in various schools try to understand the sources of human knowledge: How *can* we know? Can we, and if so, *how* can we, have access to "how things really are"? While trying to answer these questions, most philosophers at least mention the part of the human mind that holds, recalls, and synthesizes knowledge—the memory.

This chapter begins by examining memory's role in the philosophical systems developed by philosophers since Descartes—Locke, Berkeley, Hume, Kant. I then examine the ideas of some 20th-century philosophers (including Husserl, Heidegger, and Rorty) who regard memory as a source of knowledge. This trip through philosophy illustrates that modern thinkers see memory as a critical part of knowledge-making and that modern theory in rhetoric and composition would be enriched by renewed attention to memory as it is understood by philosophers today.

Rationalism Versus Empiricism

One of the oldest philosophical questions, even preceding Socrates, is whether knowledge is based primarily on sense experience or on reason. Do we know what we know because we see/feel/experience it? Or do we first know by means of some innate principles in our minds, some Forms, as Plato would call them, inherent in human understanding? Attempts to answer these questions eventually led to two schools of philosophy. Empiricists would answer "yes" to the first question; they believe that knowledge is based on the senses. Empirical knowledge is knowledge based on human observation and experience (Locke and Hume, then, are empiricists). Rationalists would answer "yes" to the second question; they believe that the foundation of all knowledge is a logical system, an underlying structure or set of basic processes present, if latent, in the human mind. Through this structure, we can know things outside of our personal physical observations.

Two adherents of rational thinking are Plato and Descartes. Plato believed in the power of memory to put him in touch with an absolute reality. For him, memory was the route to truth, even divinity. Before birth, man communes with the Forms (Beauty, Justice, Temperance, etc.). After birth, he must recollect or recover this knowledge he once had. This is Plato's Doctrine of Reminiscence (Angeles 11). Plato believed that the more he could strengthen his memory, the farther back he could see, and thus, the closer he could get to the truth. The same desire—to reach man's potential divinity—brought forth the marvelous memory theaters in the Renaissance. And Descartes' theory that we have "innate ideas"(i.e., innate knowledge of concepts such as *event, time, location,* etc.) is a classic rationalist stance.

However, it is not the rationalist tradition in philosophy that has prevailed in the 20th century. The stronger influence on the 20th century has come from the post-Cartesian empirical philosophers like Locke, Berkeley, and Hume, who rebelled against the theory of innate ideas and argued that our knowledge comes from our sense experience. Their theories began with John Locke and his "blank slate" metaphor for the human mind at birth. Locke and Hume have both been mentioned in chapter 2; here it is useful to explain their theories in more detail, for they influence so many philosophers who have followed them.

John Locke detects no evidence of innate ideas. Instead, he believes that all of our ideas come from our experience. Like Descartes, Locke separates the mind and the physical world. As we experience the physical world, we receive sensations from it, which the mind can make into ideas. These ideas we put together through recollection: Recalling and reconnecting the ideas from physical sensations gives us our mental powers of thought. Therefore, for Locke, knowledge comes from recollection and reassociation of ideas that come from experience.

Locke admits that all he knows is that he has ideas; he assumes that they somehow come from "what is," from the physical world around him. But he can really only know the contents of his mind. His successor, George Berkeley, goes even farther. Berkeley says that there is no "what is"—just what we perceive. The physical world does not exist on its own; all that exists is our ideas of the world—the world perceived. Ideas are either "imprinted on the senses" or "formed by help of memory and imagination, either compounding, dividing, or barely representing those originally perceived ..." (*A Treatise Concerning the Principles of Human Knowledge*, qtd. in Palmer, *Does* 102). This grouping—the forming, compounding, and dividing of our sensations—allows us to form recognizable patterns and create enduring ideas—the concept of a *Kleenex,* for instance, or of an *I*. These patterns make interpretation possible. And, if there is no underlying "substance," nothing but ideas, it would seem in a Berkelian philosophy that *memory* provides the glue to hold these concepts and patterns together. Memory organizes the various ideas of pieces of experience together by grouping them in ways that we recognize and that have meaning to us at the moment.

The recognizable patterns can become conventions, and one important convention is *language*. Berkeley says that language is the convention that allows individuals with different perceptions to understand and communicate with one another through words, whose meanings we share. Berkeley's ideas on language have influenced many later philosophers, including both the ordinary language philosophers and the phenomenologists of the 20th century, both of whom are discussed shortly.

According to David Hume, all we have is sense data, "a bundle or collection of different perceptions which succeed each other with an inconceivable rapidity, and are in a perceptual flux and movement" (qtd. in Palmer, *Looking* 205). There is no actual *continuity* of being, or at least no empirically observed continuity. The fact that we can see ourselves "possessed of an invariable and uninterrupted existence" at all Hume credits to memory:

As memory alone acquaints us with the continuance and extent of a succession of perceptions, it is to be considered, on that account chiefly, as the source of personal identity. Had we no memory, we should never have any notion of that succession of perceptions which constitutes our self or person. But having once acquired this notion from the operation of memory, we can extend the same beyond our memory and come to include times which we have entirely forgot. And so arises the fiction of person and personal identity. (*An Enquiry on Human Understanding*, qtd. in Castell and Borchert 569)

Hume emphasizes the notion just suggested by Berkeley's philosophy: Memory is the "glue" that holds our perceptions together. It organizes them and gives us concepts of enduring things, like the concept of oneself as a *single, continuously existing self.*

What an important role memory takes on in Hume's description! Memory is the repository of the mind, actively connecting and organizing the perceptions that enter it. Memory makes us distinguish "cloud" or "anger" or "dangerous" from the sensations that our mind takes in. Memory allows us to make knowledge out of the flux of sense data. And Hume's description has endured. In spite of the differences in the philosophical views discussed in the rest of this chapter, all appear to support a view of memory-as-the-associative-force, or memory-as-glue, which makes memory crucial in the construction of knowledge.

Immanuel Kant comes the closest to bringing the empiricists and rationalists together at the end of the 18th century. Donald Palmer explains:

> Kant rejected the empiricists' "blank slate" hypothesis on the grounds that the mind was not simply a passive receptacle of neutral sense data. However, Kant also rejected the rationalistic notion of "innate ideas" on the grounds that claiming that babies are born with ideas is just too farfetched. He replaced these innate ideas with innate *structures,* which he called "categories of the understanding" ... that imposed a kind of order on the raw data of the senses. ... This grants to the empiricists that there can be no knowledge in the absence of sensorial contribution and grants to the rationalists that sense-data alone cannot provide knowledge. (*Does* 124–125)

In other words, for Kant, there must be some structure to the way we perceive and reflect on objects that adds to our experience and organizes our sensibilities. Thus our knowledge comes from these two sources working together: sensibility and understanding. Perhaps this combination is like a similar combining of input and prior programming that occurs with a computer: The computer needs a program or processing system to direct it (understanding), which then makes sense of or organizes or works with the input we give it for each particular job (sense data). For instance, no matter how hard or how long we plunk on the keyboard, without a program to organize our plunkings, the computer will not know what to do and therefore will do nothing with our input. Meanwhile, of course, the program by itself can achieve nothing until it receives appropriate input with which to work.

Despite the general opposition of the points of view of rationalism and empiricism, a theory of memory does not need to choose one school of thought over another. Both rationalists and empiricists see human memory as playing an important role in making knowledge possible. Plato, the rationalist, pursued truth, which takes place "in communion through memory with those things the communion of which causes God to be divine." The man "who employs such memories rightly ... becomes truly perfect" (*Phaedrus* 124). Hume, the empiricist, defines ideas as "the less lively perceptions, of which we are conscious, when we *reflect* on . . . sensations" [italics added] (*Philosophical Works,* IV, qtd. in Covino, *Art,* 70). Memory is crucial to the study of knowledge from either point of view—so important that neither side could create a theory of knowledge without it. The study of memory must integrate various points of view; it defies the boundaries of particular philosophical schools, fields, or views.

The Experimental Age and the Search for New Methods

The 20th century has been a century of revolution in philosophy. It has been an age of revolt against Cartesian dualism, which juxtaposes the mind and the world. Many of the philosophers at the turn of the century believed that this subject/object dualism had been pushed too far; William James, Alfred North Whitehead, and John Dewey are examples. They were skeptical that such an impassable gulf existed between themselves and reality. It created insoluble problems in defining knowledge and finding truth. Philosophers in the 20th century explored other ways to better understand the nature of reality; these ways became the revolutionary ideas of the century.

The revolt against rationalism is examined by William Barrett in his introduction to the four-volume *Philosophy in the Twentieth Century*. Barrett speaks about rationalist idealism, an extreme rationalist stance in that it rejects the possibility that anything real could ever actually exist, but offers a critique of rationalism itself:

> it is a habit of mind woven into the very warp of Western thought and begins at the beginning of Western thought in Plato himself ... the real does not exist and what exists is not really real. What is real must remain forever unchanging and identical with itself, while what exists in the world of change and time alters from moment to moment and does not remain identical with what it was. ... Essences—that is, the eternal Ideas—precede existence. The world of the existent in time is a shadowy copy of the eternal. Such is the position toward which classical rationalism, in one form or another, always tends. (Barrett and Aiken 1:28)

And this is the position, he would say, that 20th-century philosophers attack. He quotes Whitehead's comment, "Twenty-five hundred years of Western philosophy are a series of footnotes to Plato" (27). He rephrases William James' objection to idealism: "it sweeps the dirt under the carpet and builds a picture of the world in which finite evil disappears but in which also the possibilities of chance, novelty, openness toward a future are equally stifled" (27).

Because 20th-century philosophers found themselves frustrated with the theories of the past, they obviously revolted as well against the methods of the past. As the century moved on, philosophers experimented more and more, and new methods of experimentation multiplied. Their experiments grew into competing schools of thought: phenomenology, existentialism, positivism, pragmatism, and so on. If these philosophers have had one main thrust, though, especially in the last 50 years, that thrust has been to fight off absolutism, to avoid "laying down a supposedly universal regimen for other activities which are essentially non-rational" (Aiken, in Barrett and Aiken 1:14). There is no *one* method, says modern philosophy, much less one correct view to hold. It is an age of "counter-ideology" (15). Contemporary philosopher Richard Rorty says the 20th century opposes the "Plato–Kant canon," which he defines as "the classic attempts to see everything steadily and everything whole" (*Contingency* 96).

One philosopher who envisioned 20th-century thinkers' discontent, and their dismissal of absolutes, was Friedrich Nietzsche. Nietzsche views remembering and forgetting as either having or lacking a sense of history. History weighs us down, he believes; happiness is only possible from an unhistorical point of view, like that of a beast who does not remember. Ignorance is bliss. However, Nietzsche admits the need for history, or remembering, "as a means to life" (*Use* 11). "Man can only become man by first suppressing this unhistorical element ... by the power of turning the past to the uses of the present. But an excess of history makes him flag again" (*Use* 8). If we overemphasize history, it paralyzes us into living inauthentically.

A life bound tightly in the conventions of the past has the illusion of "truth," for it acts on historical precedent. But Nietzsche questions this "truth":

> What then is truth? A movable host of metaphors, metonymies, and anthropomorphisms: in short, a sum of human relations which have been poetically and rhetorically intensified, transferred, and embellished, and which, after long usage, seem to a people to be fixed, canonical, and binding. Truths are illusions which we have forgotten are illusions ... ("On Truth" 891)

According to Nietzsche, depending on history, the accepted cultural memory of what has preceded us keeps us from action.

In the same way, language can instill a "canned" view of life. All language, Nietzsche believes, is rhetorical, and all language is metaphorical:

> we believe that we know something about the things themselves when we speak of trees, colors, snow, and flowers, yet we possess nothing but metaphors for things— metaphors which correspond in no ways to the original entities. ("On Truth" 891)

As the metaphors become widely accepted "concepts," they are less able to express an individual's perception. Thus language helps us live the "lie" that we call "truth."

We "forget" partly for self-preservation. Critic J. P. Stern says that the function of language in Nietzsche's world is "to hide the hostile nature of the universe from men in order to preserve them from destruction—at least for a little while" (67). Generally, Nietzsche seems to say that life is frightening, that we can hide from it by remembering what we are told and forgetting what we experience ourselves. But, he says, we are not really alive unless we forget what we are told (history) and remember our own experience. At the end of *The Use and Abuse of History,* Nietzsche says:

> This is a parable for each of us: he must organize the chaos in himself by "thinking himself back" to his true needs. He will want all his honesty, all the sturdiness and sincerity in his character, to help him revolt against secondhand thought, secondhand learning, secondhand action. (72)

Nietzsche seems to want us to "shift our gaze" from those of our predecessors and value our own perspective.

In talking about art in *Human, All-Too-Human*, he says that we should not try to do things just like the old masters did; rather, we should "animate the older works" with our souls: "These works can only survive through our giving them soul, and our blood alone enables them to speak to *us*." He continues:

> True, if Beethoven were suddenly to come to life and hear one of his works performed with that modern animation and nervous refinement that bring glory to our masters of execution, he would probably be silent for a long while, uncertain whether he should raise his hand to curse or to bless, but perhaps say at last: "Well, well! That is neither I nor not-I, but a third thing—it seems to me, too, something right, if not just *the* right thing. ... As our Schiller says, 'the living man is right.' So have it your own way, and let me go down again." (*Philosophy* 528)

Memory is, for Nietzsche, both constructive and destructive, a burden we must carry because we are human. It provides us sustenance but can weigh us down until we can no longer move if we let history keep adding weight to our pack.

Most contemporary philosophers, Heidegger and Rorty, for example, acknowledge basic individual perspectives, whether of field or culture or person. They accept differences in perspective and question the whole notion of there being one correct world view that we might eventually discover. The issues which command our attention today reflect this philosophical stance. For instance, multiculturalism rejects western ideology, and it favors valuing other cultural memories. So does feminism. Jean Grimshaw, in her book *Philosophy and Feminist Thinking,* says that men see reality as being objective, whereas women see it as being experiential. Her theory corresponds to that put forth by Belenky, Clinchy, Goldberger, and Tarule in *Women's Ways of Knowing.* They believe that women more often than men construct knowledge from that which is personally known or intuited; men are more apt to be objective and rule-governed.

They propose that we each have a world view based on our own perspective, which comes from experience. They propose that each new experience will be absorbed according to how the receiving mind is already informed in certain ways. There is no single or set or final way to look at things. Perspective is the key to the creation of knowledge. And if we create knowledge with minds already informed, we create knowledge through memory.

Phenomenology and Existentialism

The revolt against absolutes was apparent in one of the earliest schools of 20th-century philosophy, *phenomenology.* Phenomenologists believe that all human knowledge comes from reception and interpretation of sensory data. There is no a priori knowledge; what we might have considered a priori ideas really come just from linguistic conventions.

We can take a quick look at phenomenology by looking at the first and perhaps most important phenomenologist, Edmund Husserl. Husserl developed a theory built around "bracketing" an object—looking at it alone, free from any abstractions or presuppositions—in order to understand it. He wanted to see directly, as phenomena appear to the consciousness. "To the things themselves!" was his cry (Barrett and Aiken, 4: 137).

To Husserl, when we look at anything, our view is naturally loaded with interpretation. Only if we can remove the object from these interpretations (which are based on our experience) can we see the phenomenon itself. Then we might find some prelinguistic essence in the object itself.

Of course Husserl's efforts show that it is impossible to free the mind of interpretation; the interpreting mind is a big and unavoidable part of the creation of knowledge. *Interpretation* and *perspective* are impossible to cast off, and both happen because we have, and always rely on, our memories.

Husserl comes to an interesting conclusion when he brackets the experience of *time* (and Donald Palmer paraphrases his conclusion):

> LIVED TIME is always experienced as an eternal NOW, which is tempered by a memory of earlier "nows" (the "thenness" of the past) and is always rushing into the semi-experienceable then-ness of the future. Phenomenologically speaking, the time is always "NOW." To do anything is to do something *now*. You can never act *then*. (*Looking* 341)

Even Husserl's "now" is dependent on memories of the earlier "nows." Husserl's ideas were a step toward the even more extreme view of Heidegger, who believed there is no boundary between the mind and the world; our minds are one with the world.

Phenomenology led through Heidegger to such existentialists as Sartre, Camus, and Marcel. *Existentialists* concern themselves with how we see ourselves and with the extent of the responsibility we bear for who we are and what we do. Their common belief seems to be that "existence precedes essence"—"there is no human nature which precedes our presence in the world. All humans individually create humanity at every moment through their free acts" (Palmer, *Does* 508). This is the exact opposite of *rationalist* theory, which posits that some underlying essence precedes and governs existence.

How does the role of memory fit into these opposite views? For the rationalists, memory is at least partly structured according to a divine plan; the more we use our memories, the more we can discover this plan and our place in it. For the existentialists, however, existence is created in our own minds, and we "remember," maintain, and change it. Memory is all we have in a world which makes very little, if any, sense.

Heidegger, Being, and Memory

Martin Heidegger is usually called an existentialist philosopher. His influence on the thinking of later philosophers is strong, especially on Jean Paul Sartre and the existentialists. Also, Heidegger addresses memory quite directly. His view of memory and the value he places on it provide us with one of the most useful philosophical statements as we develop a new rhetorical theory of memory.

Heidegger opposes viewing the world as an independently existing object that is external to us, which he says has been a practice of our culture for so long, especially since Descartes. He says that our entire existence (he calls this *Dasein*, which literally means "being there") is not private and isolated but exists in-the-world; therefore we can never get far enough away from it to objectify it completely. Because Heidegger is sometimes better understood in paraphrase than in his own words, I rely some here on the words of Norman Melchert as he explains Heidegger:

> Interpretation ... is always founded on a prior understanding. ... Every interpretation *always* inevitably takes something for granted; it is worked out on some background that is not itself available for inspection and decision. (553)

This is "the hermeneutic circle: all interpretation is caught up in what is understood beforehand" (554).

For existence to be authentic, it has to understand the temporal nature of life and be based on the projecting of possibilities, therefore the future. But, Heidegger states, that depends on knowing your past:

> Only in so far as Dasein *is* as an "I-*am*-as-having-been," can Dasein come towards itself futurally in such a way that it comes *back*. Anticipations of one's uttermost and ownmost possibility is coming back understandingly to one's ownmost "been." Only so far as it is futural can Dasein *be* authentically as having been. The character of "having been" arises, in a certain way, from the future. (from *Being and Time*, 373, qtd. in Melchert 567)

In other words, "You 'are' your possibilities. But what these possibilities are depends on what you have been. You can only project yourself authentically into the future by 'coming back' to yourself as having been something" (Melchert 567). Each "being" is different, set against different backgrounds. And it is not just a bunch of moments; "it is a past that one constantly *is*" (568). Melchert concludes (from Heidegger's *Being and Time*):

> Temporality (primordial time) is the meaning of Dasein's Being—i.e. the deepest structure in Dasein through which everything else is seen to made sense. By projecting itself into future possibilities while being firmly anchored in the past, ... Dasein makes present the situation in which it acts and stretches itself along, caringly, in time. (570)

The past and the future can only be understood through the present, the reality of here and now. And perhaps here Heidegger helps us clarify the importance of memory in the line of thinking that underlies phenomenology and existentialism. Heidegger thinks recovery is everything: It is the way to "resist a kind of *ruination* in which the past sinks into oblivion":

Recovery alone produces phenomenological evidence, repeats the "primal decision" by which alone life escapes the play of masks, the carnival in which it is caught up; recovery alone resists the plunge by means of a counterthrust, a movement within life yet counter to life's own tendency to fall. Heidegger calls such recovery *counterruinance*. ... [his] first word for the overcoming of complacency and oblivion, his first word for commemorative thinking. (Krell 254)

Richard Rorty, writing about Heidegger, says that he, like Marcel Proust, "thought that if memory could retrieve what created us, that retrieval would be tantamount to becoming what one was" (*Contingency* 118). This was the point, he says, of Heidegger's *andenkendes denken*—thinking that recalls.

Heidegger rejects the idea of a subjective/objective dichotomy. We are not "subjects" trying to know a world of objects. To him, we only have existence by being in-the-world. Ideas, rememberings, truth, artistic interpretation—these things *present* themselves to us; they are revealed. Thinking is "recalling Being out of its hiddenness" (Melchert 574) in a fashion outside of ourselves that Melchert likens to the idea of the muses: This is not to Heidegger an idea of a higher being but of our willingness or ability to let Being be.

Dasein, Heidegger says, depends on discourse: "we already live in a common world with others—the public world of equipment and its structural articulation. In discourse we 'take hold' of this common legacy and express it in language" (Melchert 555).

In *On the Way to Language*, Heidegger writes that language and being are inextricably tied up together. You cannot yet have a thing until you have the language to express it: "the word alone gives being to the thing." Language he calls "the house of Being" (63).

Truth is referred to as uncovering what has already been there. For instance, Newton's laws were there before we understood them, but Newton made it possible for us to know them; he uncovered them. Heidegger talks about "things" and "language":

Is not even this "thing" what it is and the way it is in the name of its name? Certainly. ... No thing is where the word is lacking. ... The being of anything that is resides in the word. Therefore this statement holds true: Language is the house of Being. (*On the Way to Language* 62–63)

Heidegger's comingling of language, thought, and what has been, revolves around memory in a very basic sense. Heidegger talks about reflective thought, which gets its meaning through the "hidden riches" of language. He says this:

poetry and thinking not only move within the element of saying, they also owe their saying to manifold experiences with language, experiences which we have hardly noticed, let alone collected. Where we did notice and collect them, we did so without adequate regard for just what concerns us more and more closely in our present reflections: the neighborhood of poetry and thinking. (*On The Way to Language* 84)

Heidegger defines thought as the recollection of the Unthought. The Unthought resides in memory: "The Unthought is at the very heart of thought as that which affects it as intimately as possible" (Birault 168). Heidegger explains the role of memory very clearly in "What Is Called Thinking?":

> Drama and music, dance and poetry are of the womb of Mnemosyne, Dame Memory. It is plain that the word means something else than merely the psychologically demonstrable ability to retain a mental representation, an idea, of something which is past. Memory—from the Latin *memor,* mindful—has in mind something that is in the mind, thought. But when it is the name of the Mother of the Muses, "Memory" does not mean just any thought of anything that can be thought. Memory is the gathering and convergence of thought upon what everywhere demands to be thought about first of all. Memory is the gathering of recollection, thinking back. It safely keeps and keeps concealed within it that to which at each given time thought must be given before all else, in everything that essentially is, everything that appeals to us as what has being and has been in being. Memory, Mother of the Muses—the thinking back to what is to be thought is the source and ground of poesy. This is why poesy is the water that at times flows back, a recollection. Surely, as long as we take the view that logic gives us any information about what thinking is, we shall never be able to think how much all poesy rests upon thinking back, recollecting. (11)

Memory gathers and stores, and memory creates. Heidegger gives to memory the traditional mother's responsibility: to safekeep and nurture in order to encourage all possibilities for life, thought, and imagination.

Language, Philosophy, and Memory

Outside of the context of this discussion, a connection between Heidegger and Noam Chomsky might not be so clear. But in fact they share a trait common to many 20th-century philosophers, regardless of their schools or other beliefs—an interest in language and a conviction that the study of language can help answer some of the perennial philosophical questions. Thus, along with a concern for language within, say, existential philosophy, there are categories of 20th-century philosophy explicitly focused on the analysis of language: logical positivism, linguistic philosophy, and ordinary language philosophy. It is not necessary to discuss them in detail here, yet they are worth mentioning. They illustrate how rhetoric and philosophy are both concerned with how we use and respond to language. They emphasize the interrelatedness of philosophy and rhetoric in language issues, and serve as a link between the two fields. As we look at any role that memory plays in a language-based philosophy, we see that it is equally a role that it plays in rhetoric, and vice versa. The two become almost inseparable.

Noam Chomsky's linguistic philosophy is different from the other philosophies discussed here because it is a rationalistic philosophy. His "deep structure" rings of Descartes' innate ideas and of Kant's Categories of the Understanding—pre-set "programs" for organizing experience. He believes that human beings have a basic, natural grammar "hard-wired" in their brains—a sort of genetic *memoria*. He makes his case for this by showing that language is not learned through mimicking others' behavior: Children can make up an infinite number of new sentences and seem to "know" rules without being taught them. Thus he argues emphatically against the suggestion of behaviorists like B. F. Skinner that language acquisition comes from conditioned responses. Chomsky, like Plato and Descartes, looks to our minds, our memories, for structuring principles that precede our own experience. Despite the 20th-century move away from rationalism, Chomsky shows that rationalistic approaches to understanding mind and language are certainly not dead.

Although empiricists have not developed a theory of language, many of them, such as Ludwig Wittgenstein and Gilbert Ryle, do believe that the examination of language is one of the bases on which philosophical inquiry must rest. As empiricist philosophers study language, a problem they must deal with is this: How can innumerable bits of data dropping onto our initially blank slate ever end up organized, structured, and obeying rules?

Rationalism can answer that question: Descartes, for instance, would say that the mind's eye can see through the data to the underlying system; Kant would say we have a mental program to structure the data. In either case, the mind has some sort of organizational structure separate from experience, without which our experience would be a senseless flux, including our ability to make sense out of the language we hear. Empiricists, on the other hand, go back to Hume's idea: It is the memory that is the glue that holds the separate bits together, that keeps them from remaining in a senseless flux.

Ordinary language philosophy is a name associated with a variety of different empirical philosophers in the middle of the 20th century, such as John Austin, Ludwig Wittgenstein, and Gilbert Ryle. Earlier analytic philosophers like Bertrand Russell and the early Wittgenstein believed that many philosophical problems come up because we misunderstand language; therefore, we need new ways of looking at it. Their elaborate analysis of language was seen by them as getting at the "real" grammar underlying the potentially confusing "apparent" grammar of ordinary everyday language. An extreme effort at doing this was that of the logical positivists, who believed that it was their job to come up with an ideal language that could finally settle perennial philosophical problems by means of its perfect clarity.

Ordinary language philosophers do not blame language for these philosophical problems. The problems are ours, and we could overcome them if we understood and used language properly. We need to use language as tools, and like tools, words must be used in appropriate ways to be useful. A formal language system is always modified by its users. Ludwig Wittgenstein, whose later work was the inspiration for the ordinary language philosophers, said, "a word has meaning only within the stream of life" (qtd. in Palmer, *Does* 32).

The job of philosophy, according to Wittgenstein and his followers, is not to reform language, but to accurately describe its use. For words to have meaning, there must be proper and improper uses of words. The underlying rules of usage are not absolute and fixed; rather they form a complex and evolving net. These rules for using words in accordance with their meanings are changeable, overlapping, subtle, and context-dependent. Ordinary language philosophers have tried to study the subtleties in order to give us insight into what it is to know what a word means.

In this view, language, particularly the ordinary language which has developed out of our dealings with the world, allows us to understand our world. In fact, language precedes understanding. As John Searle puts it, "For Wittgenstein, there couldn't be such a thing as thinking, even such a thing as experience … apart from the use of linguistic expressions. For him, thinking is just operating with expressions; so language permeates all of thinking, and thus, all of human experience" (Magee 334). For ordinary language philosophers, it is because of the holistic way in which language hangs together in daily use that meaning exists. The meaning of each "piece" of language is derived from its use in some context. Thus, it is through the understandings and connections we each hold in our memories that meaning exists.

The subtle and often unconscious rules, habits, and conventions we hold in our own memories, based on our experience in the world, determine how we understand language and therefore what we know and how we deem things to be correctly said. Wittgenstein and Heidegger would say that we know how to use language through using it. The more we use it (experience it), the more we can sense how it is done. In other words, we *know* not just through complicated inner mental processes, but by experiencing our world. And understanding the way our experiences are joined and recollected to create this sense of what is correct, of what we know, is still not fully understood:

> There is a great deal of mental activity that remains to be accounted for. It includes a considerable part of the exercise of memory and imagination and it includes every form of sentience. (Ayer 168)

In philosophy today the interest in language has joined with a general concern for cultural pluralism that makes language study even more interesting. Language may be a subject that brings several fields together; we see it in the literary deconstruction theory of Jacques Derrida, in Michel Foucault's work in history, and in Jacques Lacan's in psychoanalysis (Palmer 380). We also see it in the writings of philosopher Richard Rorty.

The Philosophy of Richard Rorty

Richard Rorty is one of the most widely read, influential, and controversial contemporary American philosophers, a pragmatist whose ideas deliberately question much established philosophical thought. However, Rorty's ideas appear to link many modern philosophers together. His name pervades rhetoric and composition studies, partly because of his influence on the work of Kenneth Bruffee and others. Rorty's is a philosophy *based on* language; it is language, rather than "consciousness" or "mind," that represents who we are. He says this of linguistic philosophy's contribution to culture:

> It helped us to see through the Platonic notions of "objectivity," and "necessity" and "reason" and "human nature," and to substitute notions of man as a self-changing being, *capable of remaking himself by remaking his speech.* ("Epistemological" 104)

Old philosophy, he tells us, saw language as pieces of a jigsaw puzzle. Each piece would represent an appropriate way of saying something, and all the pieces could fit together and provide us with truth. Contemporary philosophy, instead of seeing its job as putting together a puzzle in its one proper form, tries to make something new that has not been considered. It is a philosophy interested in edification, or in finding *possibilities*, rather than in systematically finding final truths. It views language as a tool for edification. In using that tool we are capable of what Rorty calls *abnormal discourse,* which allows new ways of thinking about things, rather than just normal discourse, which reflects the ways we already think about them. Language then is a vehicle for change. "[W]e remake ourselves as we read more, talk more, and write more," and this remaking is the source of our education, or edification, which is through language: "the way things are said is more important than the possession of truths" (*Philosophy* 359).

Rorty, like Nietzsche, believes that the history of language is the history of metaphor, and that we constantly create *redescriptions*, which are new and not open to paraphrase; they don't yet "have a place in the language game" (*Contingency* 18). He contrasts the Platonic or positivist view of metaphor as representing a hidden reality outside us with the Romantic view of metaphor as expressing a hidden reality within us. His view is outside both of these. Influenced by "Nietzchean history of culture, and Davidsonian philosophy of language," he sees language "as we now see evolution, as new forms of life constantly killing off old forms—not to accomplish a higher purpose, but blindly" (*Contingency* 19). "Blindly" tells us that it is chance that rules, not a grand plan or a final truth to be eventually "told."

Familiarity with and comfort in normal discourse, he believes, not any "prelinguistic consciousness," is responsible for our "deep sense of how things are": This consciousness is "simply a disposition to use the language of our ancestors, to worship the corpses of their metaphors" (*Contingency* 21). And Rorty agrees with Donald Davidson, who would have us give up this effort to define our world through the language of the past: "We must give up the idea of a clearly defined shared structure which language users master and then apply to cases. ... We should give up the attempt to illuminate how we communicate by appeal to conventions" (Davidson, "A Nice Derangement of Epitaphs" qtd. in Rorty, *Contingency* 15).

Rorty is saying that the contents of our memories are shaped by the language that we have to use. Language itself is a kind of memory, acting as the lens through which we see. Therefore, we can be blinded by our language—keeping the same lens even when our vision changes—or we can modify the lens, the language, to help us see more clearly. Changing prescriptions does not usually mean radical change (we often keep the old pair of glasses around in case the new ones break); it is generally more of an evolutionary process. But every time we change the lens to better fit our need, we see more clearly, and we have new things to remember.

Using an image similar to that of the waxen tablet, Rorty refers to a person's individual heritage as "the blind impress which chance has given him" (*Contingency* 43). I think he would say that we should not look only to established patterns of life and language to deal with and make sense of our world. They will not always work, and we need to get beyond the "blind impress." In *Zen and the Art of Motorcycle Maintenance*, Robert Pirsig's hero Phaedrus had to submit to a shock treatment that forced him to forget, and therefore he had to look at the world from a new perspective, after which he spent time pursuing the ghosts of his past. Unlike Pirsig's Phaedrus, however, we should not have to submit to shock treatments and blot out our pasts to relish a fresh point of view.

Rorty talks about a "final vocabulary" that everyone carries around. He defines this as "a set of words which they employ to justify their actions, their beliefs, and their lives. ... They are the words in which we tell ... the stories of our lives" (*Contingency* 73). I think this final vocabulary, for Rorty, is akin to memory: It is these words, like certain images retained in memory, that make us what we are. And he would argue that the images or words can change; free persons can constantly redescribe themselves and the world around them. Neither language nor memory are fixed, and language, like memory, can serve as a glue to form our experiences into a sensible whole.

* * *

Nietzsche wanted us to free ourselves from history; Richard Rorty thinks we shouldn't cast off our cultural heritage. Rorty's idea of education includes "a sense of tradition." He believes there is value in Hirsch's theory of cultural literacy: the sharing of a common vocabulary and body of knowledge. He believes that

> in order to have a sense of citizenship in a country, one has to have enough historical perspective to see that this arose out of certain conditions for certain reasons and has been maintained for certain reasons against other alternatives. (Olson 7)

"Without the sense of the tradition to which you in your political role belong," Rorty says, "I don't see how anybody is going to take social criticism or suggestions for reforms seriously" (Olson 8). In other words, a cultural memory is a valuable framework for interpretation, for perspective.

We do not have to forget our pasts through shock treatments or burn our histories in order to invent, experiment, and change. In fact, it may be critical that we do not forget them.

Chapter 5

The Role of Memory in Literature and Theory

Musings

Here is a familiar picture. It's a freshman or sophomore level literature class. The teacher stands at the front of the room, asking questions about the novel that sits open on each student's desk. She looks friendly and open-minded as she asks, "What do you think about X and Y? What kind of relationship do they have?"

Heads go down. Eyes are averted. There is silence, and the silence loudly speaks: "Please don't call on me!"

Interpretation, these students would say, means figuring out what the instructor thinks about the novel. It means coming up with the right answer. But that's wrong. Interpretation means coming up with your own answer. It means making connections in your own head, with your own memories.

Here is what happens to me when I read one favorite line from Annie Dillard, who writes like Segovia plays.

> *The mind is a blue guitar*
> > *on which we improvise*
> > > *the song of the world.*

That sentence is in Living by Fiction. I've underlined it, and every time I go back and look at my underlinings I run into the wonderful line and reread it:

> *The mind is a blue guitar*
> > *on which we improvise*
> > > *the song of the world.*

When I read this line, first of all I get an immediate image of Picasso's painting, "The Old Guitarist" done in his blue period. In graduate school, I had a print of that painting thumbtacked to my wall. So did some of my friends; it was probably the number one seller among museum prints for a couple of years. I hung mine so that the man was sitting up straight, even though his head was at a funny angle. A guy I knew was more concerned about the angle of the head so he had the man lying on his back. We wondered if the music would sound the same either way.

We just assumed that the music would be as good as Picasso was with the brush.

My reading of that sentence always begins with the painting, or rather with the tattered reproduction of the painting. Then I wonder about "improvise." Improvisation is making it up, winging it. Winging it is a good term—flying free. If you could improvise the song of the world, could you be free? Could you fly? Could you even free the world and make it fly? Sometimes when you improvise you're faking it. Then is it all a lie? No. Improvisation is not a lie, it's a going beyond. It's extending the possibilities.

There isn't any one song of the world to be written. There are billions of songs. If we passed out blue guitars to everybody, would any of the songs be the same? Would my song move anyone else? How many of the songs would be played in a minor key?

> *The mind is a blue guitar*
> *on which we improvise*
> *the song of the world.*

I would like to be part of a symphony. Sometimes I would like to play other people's songs, just following along, doing my part. Sometimes I would like to be the featured soloist, and take off on a wonderful binge of improvisation that would bring the audience to its feet yelling "Bravo!" and "More!" Sometimes I would like to be the director. I would have everyone do it my way. But then I would point to another musician and my unspoken message would be "let'er rip!" and a new voice would fly off on a improvisational wind of its own. (Does that remind you of "The Benny Goodman Story"?)

The only world I have is in my mind. And I have no guitar—only the words and actions I produce. Every time I read this sentence I am inspired to use those words and actions to help create a world symphony, not a cacophony:

> *The mind is a blue guitar*
> *on which we improvise*
> *the song of the world.*

And all of this is an improvised but true statement of what happens to me when I read Annie Dillard's line. It all happens because that line makes me remember so much.

I wish I could be in a class someday where the teacher would ask, "Now what do you make of this line by Annie Dillard?" I would raise my hand.

* * *

How small the cosmos (a kangaroo's pouch would hold it), how paltry and puny in comparison to human consciousness, to a single individual recollection, and its expression in words! (Nabokov, *Speak Memory* 24)

Memory as Inspiration

Poet Amy Lowell professed to drop ideas constantly into her head, as if it were a mailbox. Months later, these ideas would reappear. Lowell always smoked cigars as she wrote, and her ideas reappeared in the smoke rings. The fact that she once bought 10,000 cigars at once shows that she was not anxious to be without that which prompted her memory and inspired her to write (Ackerman 56).

In Ernest Hemingway's posthumously published book, *The Garden of Eden*, the protagonist/writer David gives us insight into how Hemingway may have used his memory to write:

It was a good story and now he remembered how long he had intended to write it. The story had not come to him in the past few days. His memory had been inaccurate in that. It was the necessity to write it that had come to him. He knew how the story ended now. He had always known the wind and sand-scoured bones but they were gone now and he was inventing all of it. It was all true now because it happened to him as he wrote and only its bones were dead and scattered and behind him. (93–94)

"The dreadful true understanding" David aimed to write could be accomplished only by "remembering the actual things that had brought it on" (182). But a writer may not have an infinite number of opportunities to remember truly. After David's wife burns his manuscripts, their lover Marita suggests that he can write them again. "'No,' David told her. 'When it's right you can't remember. Every time you read it again it comes as a great and unbelievable surprise. ... And you're only allowed so many [good ones] in your life'" (230).

T. S. Eliot's persistent concern with time and the intermingling of the tenses show memory as an important part of the awareness that primes the creative pump:

Time past and time future
Allow but a little consciousness.
To be conscious is not to be in time
But only in time can the moment in the rose-garden,
The moment in the arbour where the rain beat,
The moment in the draughty church at smokefall
Be remembered; involved with past and future.
Only through time time is conquered.
                    ("Burnt Norton" 3)

Marcel Proust, interviewed in 1913 at the time of the publication of *Swann's Way*, says this about his work:

You see, I believe that it is almost solely from involuntary memories that the artist ought to take the central substance of his work. First of all, precisely because they are involuntary, because they form themselves, attracted by the resemblances of an identical moment, they alone have the stamp of authenticity. Also, they bring things back to us in an exactly right dosage of memory and forgetfulness. And finally, as they make us experience the same sensation in a completely different circumstance, they liberate it from all contingency, they give us its extra-temporal essence, that which is precisely the substance of the beautiful style, that general and necessary truth which the beauty of the style alone translates. (qtd. in Block and Salinger 69–70)

And Vladimir Nabokov gives his theory of memory in an interview:

imagination is a form of memory. ... An image depends on the power of association, and association is supplied and prompted by memory. When we speak of a vivid individual recollection we are paying a compliment not to our capacity of retention but to Mnemosyne's mysterious foresight in having stored up this or that element which creative imagination may use when combining it with later recollections and inventions. In this sense, both memory and imagination are a negation of time. (qtd. in Stark 91)

This chapter could easily turn into a book of tales about memory, but it need not. We are all familiar with stories from the lives and works of our favorite authors that acknowledge the debt of the past. But a handy source on my bookshelf tempted me to look in one more place for evidence of the importance of memory in writing: A friend had just given me a copy of *Poetspeak: In Their Work, About Their Work*, a 1983 anthology of 148 poems by living writers, edited by Paul B. Janeczko. Sixty-four of the poems are followed by commentary written by the poet about that poem. I read these commentaries carefully, anxious to see if many of the poets talked about memory. I was rewarded well, for 55 of the commentaries emphasized memory as the source of inspiration. Here are some examples from *Poetspeak*:

The incident stayed with me, working on my memory and imagination (the two fuse together somehow) ...(David McElroy 48)

It is a desire to bring what is mostly subconscious into some kind of open area ... (Greg Kuzma 103)

I planned it soon after revisiting a beach ... (Celeste Turner Wright 78)

Memory is each man's poet-in-residence ... (Stanley Kunitz 75)

Memory is partial, selective, vague. We can't recapture the full sense of what it was like to be alive in a certain place at a particular moment simply by remembering. That's another thing they do to you in distant places—"taking away your memory before sending you back." (Marvin Bell 162–63)

The poem is a memory of those nights ... (Peter Wild 16)

What happens in the poem comes very close to what I remember of that day ... (Vern Rutsala 14)

You tell what seems most helpful to tell, what you think about when you remember
... (William Stafford 112)

Poetry helps us remember what's brave and beautiful and sensible; to forget is to have
the life go out of us, the festival leave the community ... (John Tagliabue 138)

I wanted to write a poem from the understanding that I am a woman and indeed was
once a girl ... (Nikki Giovanni 87)

Of the nine commentaries that didn't emphasize memory specifically, William
Matthews' was called "In Memory of the Utah Stars" (52) and was therefore written
to preserve a memory, and four others referred to an event that had just happened
recently (all the others were written about fairly distant memories). Only four
commentaries completely ignored memory, for instance, Keith Wilson's comment,
"the poems simply come" (213) and Steve Orlen's "the words set me going one
day when I had no stories to tell" (188).

The commentaries in Janeczko's collection tell me again what we already know:
For many creative writers, memory is the single most important source of inspiration.

Remembering may be more than inspiration, too; it may be the means for
understanding. This theory is suggested by Norton Christie in his dissertation
Another War and Postmodern Memory: Remembering Vietnam: "to live events,
even extreme experiences like war, is not to know them; ... one must relive them
in the mind, recovering them in order to recover from them" (39). He says that the
act of remembering is "a fundamental concern" in the best art and literature to come
out of the Vietnam War (41). Both individual and cultural memory come into play,
Christie says as he discusses playwrights who write about the war:

> communal recovery is only made possible by private acts of remembering. ... "the
> very stuff of the stage" derives from conflicts played out within the memory of each
> soldier who lived the war. David Rabe established himself as a young playwright of
> promise by recasting his own Vietnam experience in dramatic form, creating charac-
> ters who in turn play out their own wars in a provocative theater of memory. The
> remembering process comes full circle, of course, when audiences bring their own
> internal conflicts to the theater where ... they may test their own perceptions against
> the concept of history presented in the play. (139–140)

Recovery is recovery? Christie says that to recover the memory is to recover
from the memory, to come to terms with it and make sense of it. (One of Christie's
chapter titles illustrates this idea: "Re/covering (from) the War.")

Experiencing an event, Christie says, is not understanding it; to understand it
one must relive it in the mind (39). Going back to the ideas of Aristotle in *De Anima*,
Christie suggests that the lived event is remembered and that the retrieval of that
memory involves imagination, which "elevates the value of the original event by
investing it with cultural validity and more sweeping powers of signification" (50).
In other words, the reconstruction of the event, perhaps altered and imagined by
the perspective of intervening time, is more valuable than the event itself for
fostering understanding.

Writing serves as "recovery" not only for wartime writers, either. Vladimir Nabokov, in *Speak, Memory* says that his life basically is not understandable, that he can only understand it through art; in other words, by writing his autobiography he can begin to make sense of his life. Through autobiography, one can discover life's "thematic designs" (Nabokov 27). Again, knowledge comes not straight from the past but from *reconstruction* of it.

The Postmodern Memory

I came to explore the wreck.
The words are purposes.
The words are maps.
I came to see the damage that was done
and the treasures that prevail.
I stroke the beam of my lamp
slowly along the flank
of something more permanent
than fish or weed

the thing I came for:
the wreck and not the story of the wreck
the thing itself and not the myth
(from "Diving into the Wreck" by Adrienne Rich)

Rich's lines might serve as a definition of postmodern memory. "Wreck" implies something from the past that has been lost, something that is to be recovered: "the thing itself and not the myth." "Wreck" also implies ruined, smashed-up, cracked-up, in pieces. Postmodern writers treat memory in various ways, but common to their work is a distrust of "the myth": the view of reality seen through the conventions and traditions of the ruling culture. The attempt to find the truth, the "something more permanent," must reject traditional ways of looking and must accept the possibility that there is nothing understandable to be found.

For example, I feel like I am diving into the wreck when I read Robert Coover's short story "The Babysitter," a story that exemplifies for me the techniques and difficulties of searching for truth in postmodern literature. In this story, Mr. and Mrs. Tucker get a babysitter for their three children and go to a party. The evening is presented in shattered fragments through the contradictory perspectives and memories of various characters. We know that things do not go well for the children or the babysitter. But we must figure out ourselves what happens that evening and who is alive or dead at the end—we must try to recover the wreck of the evening itself and not the myth. The evening itself—like our modern way of life, Coover seems to imply—emerges more clearly through these disjointed fragments than it might through the orderly, literal myth of traditional, consistent-point-of-view, chronological narration. Real life is more disjointed, and different participants in an event see and remember it differently. Although the traditional conventions of narration generally organize experience for us by focusing it in time and point-of-view, a story like Coover's refuses to do that for us and forces us to face the chaos and, if we choose, try to make sense of it.

The idea of trying to see clearly but in different ways pervades postmodern texts. Most of them demand that their readers *forget* the expected forms and continuity of traditional literature. Postmodern works are often verbal collages that emphasize the discontinuities of the world we experience. They "show the erosion of that linear, causal arrangement of words" which, according to Philip Stevick, represents an outdated literate tradition rather than the new electronic one (144). Stevick notes an important contrast between postmodern fiction and the modernist fiction which preceded it. The concept of *epiphany,* James Joyce's term for the moment of illumination, was important to the moderns; moments of epiphanies serve to make us see life more clearly. However for postmodern writers, all moments are the same. Instead of order, postmodern writers use fragmentation and chaos to "structure" their works. Our attention is then on the text itself and the experience of it rather than on any view of reality it tries to illuminate. If postmodern texts are to be "true," and if postmodern readers are to be able to read them, both must un-remember or unlearn the conventions of literature that tradition has taught its writers to respect and its readers to expect.

Although postmodern writers generally share this view of the need to forget or cast aside expectations, they otherwise treat memory differently from one another. Writers like John Barth and Jorge Luis Borges speak of memory negatively. Barth hates time and shows people stuck in time-consciousness. He associates memory with a realistic view of the world, which just causes disasters (Stark 144–145). Borges' story "Funes the Memorious" depicts a character who remembers everything. His burdensome memories fill up his mind. Funes fills up so completely with memories that he dies of congestion (Stark 33). His mind is so full of old ideas that he has no room for thought. In Alain Robbe-Grillet's novel *In the Labyrinth*, the main character, a soldier, is trying to get somewhere, carrying a box to be delivered to someone (we assume), but he cannot remember where he is going or why. He travels endlessly in the labyrinth of the city, dies at the end for no apparent reason, and is replaced. He has lost his memory; he is without meaningful images and therefore without meaning itself. His journey is filled with repetition, sameness, and attention to surface detail. If Aleksandr Luria's mnemonist "S" and Borges' Funes were immobilized by too many memories, Robbe-Grillet's soldier is done in by *lack* of memories and too much surface detail.

For Vladimir Nabokov, memory is a positive resource. John Stark brings together Nabokov's reflections on memory: Memory finds patterns (which can be reassembled by artistic creation); memory is active (it brings things to life in different frames and patterns); and memory causes vitality (it "colors" the things remembered) (92–93). Memory creates, then discovers and vitalizes patterns. In so doing, memory "does not serve time, as it does for a realist; it masters time" (93).

The important point to make here is that coming to grips with time and memory is an important concern for many postmodern writers. As they search for ways to express truth, they battle with the obstacles that time and memory put in the way. Often, they are not sure whether memory is friend or foe.

In *Reminiscence and Recreation in American Fiction*, Stacey Olster argues that postmodern writers do not completely reject the past; instead, they use it knowing that it is incomplete, fragmentary. Olster quotes Thomas Pynchon's Oedipa Mass, who refers to the attempt at knowledge as "compiled memories of clues, announcements, intimations ..." (139). Olster says that postmodern writers recreate the past, that "through the lens of remembrance and reflection, they replace the sight of the eyewitness with the insight of the more mature writer" (145). Her view seems to be that postmodern writers allow for histor*ies*—and they use them for an open-ended future, not as something closed up.

This view of plural histories is part of a postmodern awareness of what every writer and reader brings to the text. The reader, like the writer, brings to the text a unique composite of experience through which pleasure and interpretation become possible. The memory of the reader is as important in the process of interpretation as the memory of the writer is in the creation of the text.

Memory and Literary Criticism

The relationship of writer/reader/text is the primary business of literary criticism. When we look at contemporary theories and methods of criticism, we find that memory is a source of inspiration to the reader. Much of the literary criticism of the last two decades has been a reaction against New Criticism, the formalist approach to interpreting texts that prevailed through the 1960s represented by such well-known names as T. S. Eliot, I. A. Richards, Cleanth Brooks, and Robert Penn Warren. New Critical methods of approaching a text aimed to discover its meaning through its structure. For New Critics, not the author nor the reader nor the historical context were important: the structure of the text held the key to proper interpretation. Terry Eagleton's explanation of New Criticism is useful: he says that for New Critics, a poem "existed as a self-enclosed object, mysteriously intact in its own unique being ... the poem's discourse somehow 'included' reality within itself" (47). That is, the disentangling of a poem's meanings is not subjective and private; it is an objective and public task. Eagleton says, "The same impulse which stirred [New Critics] to insist on the 'objective' status of the work also led them to promote a 'strictly objective' way of analysing it" (49). Thus, the most important task for memory in interpreting a text is remembering how one has analyzed a previous work; the system remains the same.

Yet all the other "schools" of contemporary criticism put greater value on memory. In one way or another, each acknowledges the importance of the memory of the reader in the act of interpretation. I have used the categories suggested by David Richter in *The Critical Tradition: Classical Texts and Contemporary Trends*. Even though many of the names and theories in literary criticism overlap boundaries, I chose his categories as a way to expedite discussion and separate different points of view. It would be impossible to cover every facet of contemporary criticism in a short space, even within these categories. Rather than trying to be all-inclusive, I have tried to be somewhat representative and to bring out as many of the important features of contemporary criticism as possible that reflect an interest in memory.

Although most of this section is concerned with the trends of the last 20 years—psychoanalytic, poststructuralist, feminist, and reader–response criticism—the importance of memory is also evident in two longer-lived critical theories, structuralism and Marxism.

Structuralism

Structuralists believe that thought is governed by a "system" that precedes our individual consciousness, much like Plato's Forms and Jung's archetypes. Structuralists share with scientists and anthropologists the desire to find the universal structure which unites all human knowledge, "a scientific ambition to discover the codes, the rules, the systems which underlie all human and cultural practices" (Selden 66). And, for structuralists, this system is language. Semiotics—the theory of signs, the study of sign systems—is the study of language as such a structure. The language system is in memory at its deepest level, like Chomsky's linguistic competence, like the archetypes. Writers cannot use writing to express themselves but only to draw upon "that immense dictionary of language and culture which is 'always already written'" (Selden 51). It is a science of the conditions of forms, according to Barthes (Richter 921). According to Selden, because structuralism is anti-expressive, it is "anti-humanist" (51).

Structuralist theory is based partly on the differences set out in Ferdinand de Saussure's linguistic theory—the difference between *langue* and *parole*. *Parole* is the speech act, but *langue* is the underlying system that we use, the language itself. It is *langue*, the system, that structuralists want to study.

Here lies the big difference between structuralists and New Critics. Whereas New Critics were concerned with analyzing the *parole*—the words used in a particular text—the structuralists look at how that text reflects the *langue*, the system. Texts are interesting as evidence of a system, not as individually created and received works of art.

In the structuralists' view language does not reflect reality (of either the writer's mind or the world) but instead produces it (Selden 66). It actually reproduces it, if in fact the structure of reality is always already in existence. In the same way that archetypes and myths can be important thought-ordering mechanisms, so can language, and the systems work very much the same way. The system, in this case *language*, precedes thought. Structuralists Roman Jakobsen and Claude Levi-Strauss write about this in an analysis of Baudelaire's "Les Chats": "myths do not consist simply of arrangements of concepts ... they are also works of art which arouse in those who hear them ... profound aesthetic emotions. Is it possible that the two problems are but one and the same?" (878) The question suggests that both myth and language cause emotion, that emotion is actually caused not by the particular work of art but by the systems it represents. It suggests that emotional response comes from remembering concepts far larger than, but provoked by, the work of art.

Structuralist Jonathan Culler uses a term similar to Chomsky's linguistic competence to describe the ability to interpret literature—*literary competence*. Literary competence depends on knowing the conventions upon which interpretation is based. For example, three conventions for poetry are that a poem should be unified, that it should be thematically significant, and that the significance can take the form of reflection on poetry (*Structural Poetics* 177, qtd. in Richter 854). Readers become skilled at interpretation or gain literary competence through doing: "it is clear that study of one poem or novel facilitates the study of the next: one gains not only points of comparison but a sense of how to read" ("Literary Competence" 923). The system may never be clearly set out for the reader, but interpretation depends on our belief in "a coherent and comprehensive theory of literature, logically and scientifically organized, some of which the student unconsciously learns as he goes on, but the main principles of which are as yet unknown to us" (from Frye, *Anatomy of Criticism* 11, qtd. in Culler, "Literary Competence" 923.) The structure, Culler believes, comes in the reader's act of interpretation, "where the work is read against the conventions of discourse, and where one's interpretation is an account of the ways in which the work complies with or undermines our procedures for making sense of things" (928).

For structuralists, then, the word *interpretation* does not mean "looking for meaning" as much as it means "looking for the underlying principles of structure."

Narrative has an underlying structure, too: "units" of literary structure that we always expect. Vladimir Propp identifies 31 "functions" in Russian fairy tales; one, for example, is "a difficult task is proposed to the hero." And these anticipated units are pretty universal in all narration (Selden 56–57).

An important part of structuralist theory, then, appears to be a shared memory system. The system is made up of conventions that seem to precede and therefore preclude individual authors, texts, and readers. It is a common universal memory, like Plato's forms, which we search in order to unify and make sense of our literary experience.

Marxism

In general, Marxists see all texts as political. All texts are "determined by historical conditions," which are determined ultimately by social and economic factors (Richter 556). For Marxists, literature reflects social reality, and what is absent in the literature reflects what is being repressed in society ideologically: Freudian repression on a class scale.

Marxist critics concentrate on how literature reflects reality and to what extent it accepts, mediates, or resists the world view of the power structure. And as Marxist critics come to terms with this issue, they invariably concern themselves with how much the memory of the writer and reader are affected by social order in which they live. Individual critics address this issue in different ways; two contemporary critics, Fredric Jameson and Terry Eagleton, serve as examples here.

Fredric Jameson explains the Marxist view by saying that readers go to a text with all sorts of preconceptions, with the interpretations made before us and with our preconceptions about ourselves as readers. So "our object of study is less the text itself than the interpretations through which we attempt to confront and appropriate it" (Jameson 9–10). Jameson uses the term *political unconscious* for our cultural memory store; about literary interpretation he says

> we never really confront a text immediately, in all its freshness as a thing-in-itself. Rather, texts come before us as the always-already-read; we apprehend them through sedimented layers of previous interpretations, or—if the text is brand new—through the sedimented reading habits and categories developed by those inherited interpretive traditions. (9)

Jameson says that "there is nothing that is not social and historical—indeed ... everything is 'in the last analysis' political" (20). All history (he quotes Marx and Engels) is the history of class struggle—this where the political unconscious comes in.

Terry Eagleton also emphasizes the layers of unconscious ideology that pervade a text: "all those systems of representation (aesthetic, religious, judicial, and others) which shape the individual's mental picture of lived experience" (Selden 42). Literary critics and teachers, Eagleton says, have not resisted these structures. They are "custodians of the discourse. Their task is to preserve this discourse ... defend it from other forms of discourse ..." (Eagleton 201). In other words, they preserve what is in the predominant cultural memory. Eagleton suggests that literary critics would do well to adopt the practices of classical rhetoric, "[which] examined the way discourses are constructed in order to achieve certain effects" (205). Marxist criticism brings to our attention the politics implicit in the storehouse of *memoria*—rules, attitudes, assumptions, and habits—which we have inherited.

Psychoanalytic Criticism

Psychoanalytic criticism begins with the psychoanalysis of Freud, Jung, Lacan, and others and moves to literature from there. One starting place for a discussion of memory's role in psychoanalytic criticism is the differences in the theories of Freud and Jung. Freud sees one's response to literature as being triggered by the personal psyche; Jung believes it is triggered by the universal.

Freud breaks the mind into three parts, and memory is involved in all three—the conscious, which includes the memories of which we are aware; the preconscious, which includes forgotten memories and thoughts that can be brought back to our conscious; and the unconscious, which is harder to deal with because everything in it has been repressed. Yet Freud says we recreate the repressed past through fantasies and dreams, and we see evidence of this past through "meaningful mistakes—slips of the tongue, pen, or memory" (Richter 638). Freudian criticism might look at the author, the characters, or the readers. In "Creative Writing and Daydreaming," Freud describes the author's motivation in this way:

> A strong experience in the present awakens in the creative writer a memory of an earlier experience (usually belonging to his childhood) from which there now proceeds a wish which finds it fulfillment in the creative work. The work itself reveals elements of the recent provoking occasion as well as of the old memory. (655)

Freud believes that "a piece of creative writing, like a daydream, is a continuation of, and a substitute for, what was once the play of childhood" (655). All creative writing is therefore heavily based on memory.

Freud begins to move into Jungian territory when he says "it is extremely probable that myths, for instance, are distorted vestiges of the wishful fantasies of whole nations, the *secular dreams* of youthful humanity" (655).

Jung's collective unconscious we've already discussed; it is like racial memory, and we understand it through universal symbols, or archetypes, that "manifest themselves not only in myth and in dreams but in the finished art of cultures like our own in the form of symbols" (Richter 644). Jungian literary critics look for the symbols in the works of art. Artistic creation activates the archetype and probes the unconscious, Jung says in "On the Relation of Analytical Psychology to Poetry":

> The creative process, so far as we are able to follow it all, consists in the unconscious activation of an archetypal image, and in elaborating and shaping this image into the finished work. By giving it shape, the artist translates it into the language of the present, and so makes it possible for us to find our way back to the deepest springs of life. Therein lies the social significance of art: it is constantly at work educating the spirit of the age conjuring up the forms in which the age is most lacking. The unsatisfying yearning of the artist reaches back to the primordial image in the unconscious which is best fitted to compensate the inadequacy and onesidedness of the present. The artist seizes on this image, and in raising it from deepest unconsciousness he brings it into relation with conscious values, thereby transforming it until it can be accepted by the minds of his contemporaries according to their powers. (666)

What Jung is describing is similar to what Plato consciously tried to do through memory. The difference is that Jung sees the artist as unconsciously bringing up this archetype, whereas Plato describes a conscious effort to probe the unconscious. Northrop Frye's theory of literature suggests that the structure of our works of literature is archetypal as well as the content. Frye thus combines Jungian ideas with those of structuralism. Frye says that the organizing principle of art is recurrence ("Archetypes" 682), and that important natural recurrences—seasons, birth, death, and so on—accrete ritual. Yet he does not ignore the individual recurrence either: "In the middle of all this recurrence, however, is the central recurrent cycle of sleeping and waking life, the daily frustrations of the ego, the nightly awakening of a titanic self" (*Anatomy* 105). He then says, "The archetypal critic studies the poem as part of poetry, and poetry as part of the total human imitation of nature that we call civilization" (*Anatomy* 105). Thus, for Frye, a poem is never removed from the archetype-generating forces around it—it is never separate from the memory systems that inform it.

Contemporary French psychoanalyst Jacques Lacan believes that it is language that creates the unconscious. As a human being begins to speak, he puts himself into a "pre-existing symbolic order," submits to it, and allows his life to be organized by it. "It is the particular privilege of man the language user to remain oblivious, while making things with words, of the extent to which words have made, and continue to make, him" (Bowie 109). According to Lacan, it is only when we reach a stage of development that allows us to use language that we have desires that are unmet and therefore something to repress [forget]. To Lacan, the unconscious is not generated by something sexual but by something absent, either a mere lack or a need (Richter 648). Although his unconscious is like a language, it is like a foreign tongue: "the discourse of the Other" (Richter 648). Malcolm Bowie discusses the importance Lacan places on literature: "students of the human mind wishing to grapple with the 'problem of meaning' could not do better than serve an apprenticeship as students of literature. For literature exposes and dramatises the refractory linguistic medium in which all production of meaning takes place" (140). The two major functions of literature that Bowie emphasizes both have to do with memory. Literature thus provides a common memory storehouse.

Two 1987 issues of *College English* feature articles about psychoanalysis and criticism, focusing on the application of psychoanalysis to classroom practices. A psychoanalytic reading of texts can benefit students, we are told. These articles suggest that the writing teacher can help students get beyond conscious memory to the unconscious memory. They suggest that stimulating the unconscious is an important part of interpretation:

> A psychoanalytical reading ... sees conscious attitudes and beliefs as unstable constructions resulting from an ongoing struggle with conflicting forces within the self. Consciousness is only one part of a complex signifying process. (Johnson and Garber 631)

Getting students beyond conscious attitudes and beliefs is an important job of the teacher:

> the systematic bringing to discourse of unconscious thoughts (or resistance to thought) is the teacher's primary task. Our difficulties in teaching students to think consciously often stem from a failure to engage and verbalize the unconscious conceptual grammars of which we, and our students, are the subjects. ... There is a "pedagogical unconscious," then, informing our educational performance. (Jay 789)

The use of psychoanalytic approaches in the classroom helps probe the psyches (the memories) of readers, writers, and characters and thus enhances possibilities for interpretation.

Psychoanalytic criticism brings into focus the ways in which the storehouses of both personal and cultural memory influence the reading of the text. For the psychoanalytic critic, the memory of the reader determines interpretation.

Poststructuralism

Poststructuralism is an attack on structuralism meant "to generate skepticism about most of the doctrines we unquestioningly accept" (Richter 943). It tells us just what postmodern literature tells us—there is no center.

Poststructuralists do not believe in any kind of underlying universal structure in language or anything else. Language can only be considered in its social context, as *discourse*, or language-in-use (Selden 76).

Unlike structuralists, poststructuralists do not believe in something like an overriding memory system. Their various approaches to language and literature all seem to say that nothing is privileged but maybe the individual mind/memory of the interpreter as he or she interacts with texts.

According to poststructuralists, authors/texts/other texts/readers should all come together with a sense of interactive free play. Poststructuralists work hard to deemphasize both the author and the text as focal points for interpretation and to give more latitude to the reader. In *The Pleasure of the Text*, Roland Barthes suggests that "[t]he general pleasure of the text is whatever exceeds a single transparent meaning. As we read, we see a connection, an echo, or a reference, and this disruption of the text's innocent, linear, flow gives pleasure" (Selden 79). It is that which comes from our own memories as readers that gives the pleasure. This interpretation is similar to Jacques Derrida's free play, which he says comes from the loss of a center; it is "Nietzschean affirmation—the joyous affirmation of the freeplay of the world and without truth, without origin, offered to an active interpretation. ... In absolute chance, affirmation also surrenders itself to *genetic* indetermination, to the *seminal* adventure of the trace" ("Structure, Sign, and Play" 970). This active interpretation is not interpretation-in-search-of-the-origin. It is based on the memory of the individual, not the dominant culture.

Richard Rorty compares Derrida to Proust: Derrida, like Proust, has "extended the bounds of possibility" by "incessantly recontextualizing whatever memory brings back" (*Contingency* 137). Meaning comes from *our* reading, *our* context. In "Plato's Pharmacy," Derrida suggests that this kind of reading has been stifled: in reading Plato's *Phaedrus*, we have assumed *pharmakon* to mean "drug," yet it has many possible meanings, from drug to poison to remedy to medicine, and accepting any of these various meanings changes the nature of our interpretation. For Derrida, we must be made to look for "differance," for the gap between language and what it signifies. These gaps—what is not there—become the basis for new interpretative possibilities, for these gaps allow us to fill in with our own meanings.

For Julia Kristeva, such possibilities lie in poetic language. Poetic language allows opportunities to disrupt authoritarian discourses by liberating the unconscious and by allowing the flux of impulses which she calls desire to come into play. In *Revolution in Poetic Language,* Kristeva says that the signifying process is made up of the "semiotic" ("drives and their articulations") (43) and the "symbolic" (meaning which is imposed by the social realm). The value of poetic language to Kristeva is that it "introduces the subversive openness of the semiotic 'across' society's 'closed' symbolic order" (Selden 83). Poetic language can disrupt the ruling discourse. Both the way it is written and the response it seeks are "outside 'monumental history'" (Kristeva 51).

Poststructuralist theorists believe that interpretation is a creative act which occurs as the reader interacts with the text, allowing memory to join in and help form the interpretation. This memory-related creativity is "rewriting": Interpretation means that the reader "rewrites" the text. "Rewriting," like writing, is driven by memory.

Memory for poststructuralists is not just the past but a blend of past, presen,t and future; memory is a reconstruction. In *Blindness and Insight: Essays in the Rhetoric of Contemporary Criticism*, Paul de Man states that

> The *instant de passage* supplants memory or, to be more precise, supplants the naive illusion that memory would be capable of conquering the distance that separates the present from past moment. ... Only the poetic mind can gather scattered fragments of time into a single moment and endow it with generative power. (qtd. in Krell 292)

Derrida says in *Memoires: for Paul de Man* that "Memory stays with traces, in order to 'preserve' them, but traces of a past that has never been present, traces which themselves never occupy the form of presence and always remain, as it were, to come—come from the future, from the *to come*" (58). The concept of the *trace* encourages us to look at memory as unpredictable, unbidden, individualized, and incomplete. We may not know what's there/not there, but the traces (and the gaps—the forgotten—which are inevitably a part of the concept of trace) are the basis on which our interpretation of the world takes place.

The three speeches that comprise *Memoires: for Paul de Man* are founded on the idea that memory, Mnemosyne, is at the foundation of all thought of past, present, and future. To Derrida, deconstruction (the strand of poststructuralism for which he has been a most influential spokesman) depends on our ability to separate "artificial memory" (his list includes habitat, culture, writing, informatization, technosciences) from "interior" memory, or thought (Derrida, *Memoires* 107). According to David Krell in his research of the place of memory in modern thought, traditional modes of memory, represented by the classical waxen tablet image, have broken down. New ways of thinking about memory, like Derrida's, show memory as being always on the verge of a never present past (7). Memory is not a stable repository of the past; instead it is reconstructive and creative, dependent on past, present, and future.

Deconstruction is the attempt to expose the "powerful and yet unspoken assumptions that have blinded Westerners to the deceptive nature of speech and writing and their role in human activities" (Crowley, *Teacher's* xvi). This Derrida calls "the metaphysics of presence," the idea that "minds can correctly perceive and experience the world because they have a natural representative relation to it" and they have language through which they can re-present it (Crowley, *Teacher's* 3). In the attempt to rid our minds of this cultural brainwashing, deconstructionists such as

Derrida hope to bring us back to pure thought. Our memories then will be cleared of the contamination from outside, and will be free to expose their "differance." Arnold and Cathy Davidson define the deconstructive critic as one who

> fully acknowledges the subjective aspect of reading a text (or writing one, for that matter), and, instead of attempting to make a particular reading seem somehow universal, emphasizes the *value* of individuality, plurality, subjectivity, and particularity in all responses to texts and in texts themselves. (83)

In other words, trusting the interior memory is superior to trusting the memory (assumptions/conventions/values) prescribed by the dominant culture.

The memory prescribed by the dominant culture is what Sharon Crowley calls "the powerful and yet unspoken assumptions" (*Teacher's* xvi). Michel Foucault calls it the "positive Unconscious," which, Raman Selden explains, grows out of the particular discursive practices of an era or a field.

> History is this disconnected range of discursive practices. Each practice is a set of rules and procedures governing writing and thinking in a particular field. These rules govern by exclusion and regulation. Taken together the fields form a culture's "archive," its "positive Unconscious." (101)

We cannot understand our own, however, only those from which we are detached. Foucault's ideas have been a source of inspiration to many literary critics as they challenge the prevailing "truths" created by the rules and procedures of the dominant culture—by the discourse of the community in power. His ideas suggest how influential the language of the culture can be in determining what and how we remember, know, and believe.

The New Historicist critics base their study of literature on Foucault's positive Unconscious. They study literature in the culture of its period. Unlike earlier literary studies that based a piece of work in its culture, New Historicism looks not for truth but for stories of the time. History is "always a matter of telling a story about the time" (Selden 105). Historian Hayden White's explanation of his own view of history may clarify the New Historicist way of thinking. To White, all of history is "a verbal structure in the form of a narrative prose discourse":

> Histories (and philosophies of history as well) combine a certain amount of "data," theoretical concepts for explaining these data, and a narrative structure for their presentation as an icon of sets of events presumed to have occurred in times past. In addition, I maintain, they contain a deep structural content which is generally poetic, and specifically linguistic, in nature, and which serves as the precritically accepted paradigm of what a distinctively "historical" explanation should be. This paradigm functions as the "metahistorical" element in all historical works. (ix)

Such a view of history-as-stories prizes the individual memory and the reconstruction of memories as no objective view of history has ever done.

Feminist Criticism

Feminist criticism examines the effects of gender on reading and writing. Its central precept is that the feminine unconscious has been repressed by culture throughout time. To feminist critics, women have been coerced into ways of thinking and acting by a male-dominated culture and discourse and by a male-produced stereotype that has limited their roles. The repression is both individual and collective. Feminist critics reject this tradition, encourage women to read and write as women, and educate their readers about gender differences in ways of reading and writing. Feminist critics emphasize the importance of memory both as a suppressor of and an instigator of feminist language and thinking.

In feminist theory, the canon is partly responsible for the collective repression of women. The canon, which is our shared literary tradition, our cultural memory, is a male tradition. The works that comprise the canon have been written by and chosen by men. Women have no canon, but only a lack of tradition. Annette Kolodny explains the significance of this lack of tradition in "A Map for Rereading: Gender and the Interpretation of Literary Texts." She has been talking about Charlotte Perkins Gilman's story, "The Yellow Wallpaper":

> That it did not—nor did any other woman's fiction become canonical in the United States—meant that, again and again, each woman had to confront anew her bleak premonition that, both as writers and readers, women too easily became isolated islands of symbolic significance, available only to, and decipherable only by, one another. If any Bloomsian "meaning" wanders around between women's texts, therefore, it must be precisely this shared apprehension. (54–55)

If there is no common context, no shared memory, there is no ability to read. Kolodny quotes Norman Mailer's "terrible confession" as the epitome of this inability: "I have nothing to say about any of the talented women who write today.... I do not seem able to read them" (60). Mailer's attitude is an example of what she calls "gender-inflicted interpretative strategies responsible for our mutual misreadings, and even misprisions, across sex lines" (54).

Women have been taught to read from a male perspective. But Judith Fetterley, in *The Resisting Reader*, says that reading-like-a-man adds to women's powerlessness; the first act of a feminist critic must be resistance rather than assent. She must look at the text with fresh eyes. Using Adrienne Rich's term, Fetterley calls this "re-vision" (viii). The whole idea of resistance in learning, part of but certainly much larger than feminist criticism, suggests that resistance is a purposeful not-remembering. It can work both for and against us: As resisting learners in a traditional setting, we pay the consequences when we refuse to remember what is expected of us. Yet as purposely resistant readers, we can challenge mainstream expectations by "forgetting" how we are "supposed to" read, by getting beyond present consciousness (knowing how to read like a man, or like a New Critic) to our own unconscious (reading our own ways and using our own memories to make connections).

Yet the supposition that resistance is purposeful brings up questions of its own. Do we always know when we are resisting and when we are surrendering to the status quo? Can we separate the personal unconscious from the political or cultural unconscious enough to make insightful decisions about resistance? Memory is so enigmatic that absolute answers to these questions are impossible.

Entrapped in the language and culture of men, women have repressed or forgotten their own needs and drives, and the result has been silence: "Muffled throughout their histories, they have lived in dreams, in bodies (though muted), in silences, in aphonic revolts" (Cixous 886). Fetterley says this of woman:

> Hemmed about with myths and images and dogmas and definitions and laws and strictures and God and Man, and *fear* and *fear* and *fear*, she is deceived into believing the theory about the bit of flesh and the bite of apple and is kept from knowing of what she is bereft. Her condition is isolation. (ix)

This silence or muteness is also seen as a blank slate: The woman is a blank slate upon which man writes. Susan Gubar refers to this as the "model of the pen/penis writing on the virgin page" (295). Any ideas a woman might have of herself—as person or writer—are replaced by the inscription of the male culture upon her.

Feminist critics urge women to reawaken their unconsciousnesses and to invent a new language by remembering a forgotten past. Helene Cixous believes that

> Women must write through their bodies, they must invent the impregnable language that will wreck partitions, classes, and rhetorics, regulations and codes, they must submerge, cut through, get beyond the ultimate reserve-discourse, including the one that laughs at the idea of pronouncing the word "Silence." (886)

Women must explore their own unconsciousnesses and create their own language. By doing so, they can achieve power. In Julia Kristeva's work, "woman is the silence of the 'unconscious' which precedes discourse. She is the 'Other,' which stands outside and threatens to disrupt the conscious (rational) order of speech" (Selden 150). Mary Eagleton, in *Feminist Literary Theory: A Reader*, explains that many theorists believe that it is "feminine writing" (not necessarily but probably coming from women) that will disrupt the tradition of male language. Her examples are these:

> Cixous points to "historico–cultural reasons"; Heath claims that "the force of their experience" will provoke such writing; Eagleton speaks of "complex psychoanalytical reasons," while Kristeva privileges the link between the semiotic and the close contact between the child and the mother's body. (202)

Notice that all these examples in Eagleton's passage involve memory—history, culture, experience, the psyche, the mother. The implication is that through the force of memory, feminine writing will have the power to break down the masculine tradition. And memory is the main liberatory factor for those in doubly marginal situations, such as lesbians or Black women. Eagleton suggests that these women dispute and expose "the dominant literary values" by seeking out "their own traditions, looking for names, for a history, for foremothers" (3). In other words, they search in their own memories (as Alice Walker suggests, in search of our mothers' gardens) for the voices that will have the power to shatter the status quo.

This last point is clearly made by Gayle Greene in her article "Feminist Fiction and the Uses of Memory." Greene says that memory "is especially important to anyone who cares about change, for forgetting dooms us to repetition; and it is of particular importance to feminists" (291). Women's political and historical past has been lost, forgotten, erased. Greene documents the attempts of contemporary feminist writers to rediscover what it means to be human and to be female. Their characters do this consciousness-raising through re-membering, "a bringing to mind of repressed parts of the self and experience" (300). The process is often expressed in archaeological terms: digging, excavating, or, like the character in Adrienne Rich's poem excerpted earlier, diving into the wreck. Such excavating, Greene tells us, gives us a new kind of memory that allows us "to construct alternatives for the future" (300–301). It is "a powerful impulse toward political action" (Jane Flax, "Re-Membering the Selves: Is the Repressed Gendered?" qtd. in Greene 301).

Reader–Response Criticism

Reader–response criticism is the least text-oriented of the varieties of criticism presented here. It considers what the reader brings to the text, a notion that was voiced little by critics until the last 20 years and is now causing radical changes in literary criticism. Reader–response's early champion was Louise Rosenblatt, whose 1938 book *Literature as Exploration* is a major defense of the reader. According to Rosenblatt, readers bring their own personal experiences to the text and, in doing so, modify both. The experience is a transaction between reader and text:

> The reader's fund of relevant memories makes possible any reading at all. Without linkage with the past experiences and present interests of the reader, he will not be prepared to bring it to life. Past literary experiences make up an important part of this equipment which the reader brings to literature, but these have usually been empha- sized to the exclusion of other elements derived from general life experience. (81)

To Rosenblatt, the reader must have not only "intellectual potentialities" but "emotional readiness" as well for reading experience to mean anything (82). This emotional readiness was ignored until the last 20 years or so. Wayne Booth appears to be addressing emotional readiness as early as 1961 when, in *The Rhetoric of Fiction*, he says that in reading *King Lear*, "my work is not that of figuring out, of calculating allusions, of unravelling intentions. It is the work of raising myself to the height required to experience the imaginative and emotional complexities of Lear's tragedy" (304). Acknowledging the value of the emotional response means valuing what personal memory and experience bring to reading. But we cannot forget the other role that memory plays. School teaches us how to read a piece of literature; it teaches us the conventions of each genre. This knowledge is Jonathan Culler's "literary competence": "to read a text as literature is not to make up one's mind *a tabula rasa* and approach it without preconceptions; one must bring to it an implicit understanding of the operations of literary discourse which tells one what to look for" (918). How much we have internalized, or memorized, about these conventions determines how successful we are in joining the discourse of the critical community. This emphasis on previous reading experiences, Rosenblatt and reader–response advocates would say, has devalued the emotional response to literature.

Hans Robert Jauss' reception theory of literature assumes that the text itself calls up these memories: "A literary work ... predisposes its audience to a very specific kind of reception by announcements, overt and covert signals, familiar characteristics, or implicit allusions. It awakens memories of that which was already read" (1202).

However, the majority of reader–response critics today follow Rosenblatt's lead and emphasize the reader as much as or more than the text. Wolfgang Iser, in "The Reading Process: A Phenomenological Approach" (from *The Implied Reader*), reiterates the theme of reading as a transaction: "The convergence of text and reader brings the literary work into existence" (1219). He clearly explains the importance of memory in the reading process:

> Whatever we read sinks into our memory and is foreshortened. It may later be evoked again and set against a different background with the result that the reader is enabled to develop hitherto unforeseeable connections. The memory evoked, however, can never reassume its original shape, for this would mean that memory and perception were identical, which is manifestly not so. The new background brings to light new aspects of what we had committed to memory; conversely these, in turn, shed their light on the new background, thus arousing more complex anticipations. Thus, the reader, in establishing these interrelationships between past, present, and future, actually causes the text to reveal its potential multiplicity of connections. (1222)

No text is complete; every text contains "gaps." The reader completes the text, filling in the gaps left by the text. (Remember Derrida's idea of "gaps," his suggestions of various ways to read *pharmakon* in "Plato's Pharmacy.") Reading is an activity that is "a sort of kaleidoscope of perspectives, preintentions, recollections"; it is done through a process of "anticipation and retrospection" (1222).

Readers who can't bring their own feelings or reactions to a text get too close to it, Elizabeth Flynn believes. In "Gender and Reading" she gives a long example of a student paper which starts with these two sentences: "'Araby' is another story that has great inner meaning. Each paragraph has some meaning; for example, the first paragraph has some deep inner meaning about what the houses represented." The rest of the analysis is similar. Flynn says:

This student was so close to the textual details that he could make no sense of them; he brought little of his past experiences to bear on the text and so could gain no critical distance from it. ... For him the text is a reservoir of hidden meanings rather than a system of signs to be acted on. (238)

The reader detached himself from his own storehouse of memories that might have come to bear on his reading of the text. Flynn even suggests that women may be better readers than men because of "a willingness to listen, a sensitivity to emotional nuance, an ability to empathize with and yet judge" (252). These are traits related to trusting personal experience (thus personal memories), akin to the more "womanly" ways of knowing that Belenky, Clinchy, Goldberger, and Tarule relate in *Women's Ways of Knowing*: receiving knowledge through listening to others and paying attention to the subjective inner voice.

The suggestion that certain traits or ways of reading are gender-specific is not an agreeable idea to everyone. Still, it is worth noting, as it represents an effort to identify modes of thought, discourse, and response that are foreign to the dominant tradition. If the suggestion is in itself too categorical, too much an attempt to objectify and generalize, it shows the need to look at each reader as having the potential for a different, subjective response to what she *or* he reads.

Subjectivity is inescapable, anyway, David Bleich asserts in *Subjective Criticism*: "any meaning is a construction whose topical influence and objectivity need no longer deny its subjective origins and character" (237). Bleich begins his book with the example set forth by Thomas S. Kuhn in *The Structure of Scientific Revolutions*. In Bleich's words, "[t]he paradigmatic perception of reality at any moment in history *is* the reality at that time" and therefore "reality is invented and not observed or discovered by human beings" (11). Language is an important maker of our perceptions of reality, and Bleich believes that one of the important roles of a subjective paradigm is to look at the way language shapes thought. This refrain is beginning to sound familiar as we look at contemporary thought and literary criticism: we must be aware of the ways in which the prevailing discourse defines and limits our thoughts and actions. Acknowledging subjectivity at the cultural, community, and personal levels allows us to better do what Bleich assumes is "our most urgent motivation": to understand ourselves (297). And in English, he says, "the 'real' objects are words and texts; the symbolic objects are language and literature. The subject is people, who speak, read, and write" (298).

In *Readings and Feelings: An Introduction to Subjective Criticism*, Bleich suggests that students recreate the text (by reading it) at three levels—perception, affective response, and associative response. They rephrase it in their own words (which represent the subjective perceptions of it), they tell how it makes them feel, and they associate the reading with other experiences they know. Each student reworks the text "according to the demands of his personality at the time of the reading" (48). And the reworking means using the subjective lens of memory at each of the three levels of response.

Bleich is credited by Norman Holland for reversing the traditional critical process: Traditionally, we analyze the text to understand the responses. Bleich has us analyze the responses to understand the text (Holland 12). And Holland, in his work *5 Readers Reading*, agrees with Bleich's assessment that readers recreate a text in terms of their own personality: "each reader absorbs what he reads as raw material from which to create one more variation on his continuing theme" (201). Identification with a text makes the response deeper, Holland believes, but this is not identification in any superficial sense. Instead, it is "a total re-creation of our psychological processes. ... We 'identify'—in the literary sense" (205).

This identification with the text occurs at the most basic level—the words themselves. Richard Marius suggests:

> To use language is to use tropes, figures, images. If we know anything about language now, we know that it cannot be ... a clear pane of glass through which a writer shows readers reality. Words are things in themselves, figures of something beyond, and yet in the figure lies their power, for the figure calls up our diverse treasures of memory, conscious and subconscious, and makes us accept the necessary fiction of any literary communication: that the writer is somehow bone of our bone and flesh of our flesh, that we share human being with the writer in a world of time and place and sense experience, that we may begin with the sharing and go along on the journey that the writer leads. (6)

The same kind of sharing takes place between readers to create group meaning, Norman Holland says. We join our private subjective selves to the outside world by responding to it and sharing it. Consensus comes from this sharing:

> It is only by being different from one another that we can have the experience of sharing. Your having a personal style makes it possible for you to take in something that I have said and make it your own. Thus, paradoxically, only by beginning with different subjectivities can we arrive at that consensus about experience that constitutes all the objectivity subjective beings can have. If we were not different and therefore subjective, we could not sense reality at all—we would simply be compelled by it. (231)

It is our own personality, made up of our own memories, that is the basis of sharing and consensus—the basis of enjoying and understanding a text as well as the basis of creating and maintaining a culture.

* * *

By rejecting New Criticism and moving beyond Structuralism, literary critics in the past 20 years have validated the personal memory more emphatically than in any other period of literary history. In fact, as explanatory texts categorize the various critical theories and specify their differences, one important similarity seems to be ignored: contemporary literary criticism in all its incarnations regards memory as the storehouse of experience through which not only invention but also *interpretation* becomes possible.

Interpretation is an act of memory. We interpret based on our relationship to the prevailing discourse of the time and field, and based on the relationship between our cultural and personal histories. Our interpretation varies with our closeness to or distance from that prevailing discourse. Interpretation depends on our own unconscious, whether it be filled with Freudian or Kristevan or some other processes, and on our willingness to deal with its contents as they relate to the prevailing culture. In other words, interpretation depends on what is in my past and how willing I am to retain, examine, or discard it.

Modern literary criticism acknowledges the likely opposition between individual and cultural memory. The culture fills our memories with ideas, conventions, and regulations which may be different from what is in our interior memories. For instance, imagine the content of the majority of essays in a class of college freshmen told to write about high school graduation. Our culture tells us this event is supposed to be interpreted in a certain way—significant, exciting, nostalgic. Most of the writers will write it up this way, and most peer readers will affirm it. If these student writers trusted their personal memories more than the cultural norm, few of them would be likely to really remember graduation day just that way.

The more my personal memory has been involved in reading a text, the more I can talk about that text. I can talk about a character more intelligently if I can identify/sympathize with him or her. even when I read a memo at work from a colleague, and I know previous facts that change the meaning or render the tone false, I interpret the words—and the gaps—at an entirely different level than someone without those extra facts.

If we accept the notion that interpretation is completely dependent on both personal and cultural memory, on both the conscious and the unconscious past, we as teachers must help students understand the importance of memory in interpretation. We must help them to understand the power and the place of the personal and the cultural memory, and we must help them to use both. We must encourage them to interpret. They do not always have to know where, why, or when they enter the text, but they need to know that various entries and responses can be valid.

Although Wayne Booth does not use the word *memory* in this excerpt from *Critical Understanding: The Powers and Limits of Pluralism*, he speaks out for the multiple perspectives that come when we listen to our own memories and encourage others to listen to theirs:

Let the voices multiply; the more voices we have the more truth will finally emerge.

Critics have always quarreled. There could be no genuine criticism if they stopped quarreling, because criticism can be practiced only by free agents whose conclusions depend on perceptions, feelings and thoughts that can never come in a single mold. (4)

Chapter 6

Memory, Rhetoric, and the Teaching of Writing

Musings

We are trying to decide where to go for our family summer vacation. We have the atlas and the calendar out on the kitchen table, and the five of us are intently peering at the whole country in front of us.

"We definitely want to get out of the state, right?" Kirk asked us.

"Yes!" four voices affirmed in unison.

"How about New England," I suggested. "I haven't been there since I was a kid, and it's so pretty."

"What's there?" Kent asked.

"Beautiful countryside, the Atlantic Ocean, Boston, history ... "

Kirk interrupted me. "Let's save New England for fall sometime. It's so beautiful then. Kids, you won't believe how much more colorful New England falls are than ours."

"We could go back to California," Hannah chimed in. "That was so much fun last year!"

"No! It was great, but not again. Let's go some place new," Warren insisted.

"I'd love to try some salmon fishing up in the Northwest." Kirk turned a few pages in the atlas. "We might even go up to British Columbia."

"What's there?" Kent asked again.

"Great salmon fishing, great trout fishing, rugged countryside, and lots of places to go on ferries."

Hannah liked that idea. "Ferryboats sound neat! Let's do that."

I winced. "Hey, guys, no regular trout fishing, okay? We can do that here any time. If we're going to go so far from home, let's enjoy what that part of the country has to offer."

"Isn't that where Victoria is?" Warren asked, "Isn't that the place that's still like an old-fashioned city in England?"

It didn't take much longer before the summer vacation was set and British Columbia was the unanimous choice. Everybody found promise of new adventure there.

Planning a vacation is much like choosing a new novel to read. I'm always looking for the promise of a new adventure. Then, the adventure isn't ferryboats or autumn leaves; it's a refreshing style, a sense of humor, an uncommon perspective, an eye for detail. Take, for instance, Love in the Time of Cholera by Garcia Marquez. It has all of those. Every time I think back to the ending of the book, I am again as delighted as when I read it. Or take Ellen Gilchrist's short stories in Light Can Be Both Wave and Particle. The collection is like a dessert tray, each story a different and wonderful treat.

Now I turn to my task at hand—grading the papers of my freshman students. And here is my very serious question: How can I teach so that those papers become more of an adventure, more like vacation or good novels or dessert?

*   *   *

Behind every word a whole world is hidden that must be imagined. Actually, every word has a great burden of memories, not only just of one person but of all mankind. Take a word such as bread, or war; take a word such as chair, or bed or Heaven. Behind every word is a whole world. (Heinrich Boll, qtd. in Murray, *Shoptalk* 160)

Memory is reclaiming its place of importance in the theories of many scholars in our own discipline: Rhetoricians, teachers of writing, and composition theorists, many of whom fit all three labels. The enigma that is the human memory sometimes goes by different names, but in rhetoric and composition today, it is more and more frequently regarded as a generative force in composing.

Memory's Place in a Revisionist Rhetoric

In the early 1980s, Maxine Hairston suggested that research in composition was in the first stages of a paradigm shift analogous to Thomas Kuhn's notion of scientific revolutions. A prominent feature of the "shift," she states, is "the move to a process-centered theory of teaching writing" (77). In "The Winds of Change," she hints at the burgeoning interest in memory:

What are we finding out? One point that is becoming clear is that writing is an act of discovery for both skilled and unskilled writers; most writers have only a partial notion of what they want to say when they begin to write, and their ideas develop in the process of writing. They develop their topics intuitively, not methodically. (85)

Ideas are generated and we discover what we want to say—we activate our memory stores through writing itself.

Her implicit suggestion for a "revisionist" view of writing is important to the study of memory, for in the revision (re-vision, re-collection) of old interpretation comes a new understanding of the importance of memory. William Covino's *The Art of Wondering: A Revisionist Return to the History of Rhetoric* is a good example of revisionist rhetorical theory. Covino argues that techniques, rules, and formulas for finished discourse fill our handbooks, but forgotten are those interpretations of rhetoric as an art of wondering, "of writing as a mode of *avoiding* rather than *intending* closure" (9). In reviewing some of the classic writers on rhetoric, he points to the works of Plato, Montaigne, Hume, and Vico, who encourage ambiguity and wondering in rhetoric. As discussed in chapter 2, Covino believes memory to be an important part of rhetoric. In his discussion of Giambattista Vico, he states, "Invention is informed by memory and provoked by wonder" (61). In a book that "revises" rhetoric to be the art of wondering, he sees memory as wonder's partner in invention. He relates Vico to the rhetoric he envisions today:

> memory reconsidered in its Vichian associations becomes an element that cannot be dismissed from modern, generative rhetoric. Memory is not merely the replication of experience; it is for Vico experience imagined and invented, altered and arranged, recollected and re-associated. ... Memory is a faculty that makes experience. ... Experience becomes the resource of imagination and invention under the aegis of wonder. (62)

Covino ends his book with a discussion of the inhibiting factors of language itself: We cannot have ideas and attitudes that cannot be expressed in available language. The prevailing modes of discourse structure our experience and thus our thinking. Covino suggests that we move beyond the bounds of this imposed structure as much as possible: We revise and reinvent "a forgotten rhetoric of ambiguity" (9), which is the art of wondering. For him this becomes a rhetoric of multiple perspectives, innovation, and thick description. It is a rhetoric that "celebrates the generative power of the imagination" (128) and therefore the individual memory.

Covino's textbook, *Forms of Writing, A Dialogue on Writing, for Writers*, takes a rhetoric of wonder into the classroom. In his introduction, he asks students to take part in "the *exploration* that writing and reading and serious discussion can provide us, and the *community* that we create whenever we add other voices to our own" (xv). Whether or not students read and take his introduction seriously, it is up to us as teachers to provide the atmosphere for exploration and community.

One of the most vocal advocates of returning to a five-part-canon system of rhetoric, Kathleen Welch argues that both memory and delivery are crucial in modern rhetoric. In both "The Platonic Paradox: Plato's Rhetoric in Contemporary Rhetoric and Composition Studies" and the more recent *The Contemporary Recep-*

tion of Classical Rhetoric: Appropriations of Ancient Discourse, Welch particularly advocates a revisionist look at Plato's place in rhetoric. She believes that the last generation has read Plato as being antirhetoric because he attacks sophistic rhetoric. This is a mistake, she says, because without Plato we promote technical rhetoric and lose dialectic, which requires memory and delivery. Revision for Welch means looking again at Plato's philosophical rhetoric and at the close alliance of Greek and Roman rhetoric with politics and culture. A technical rhetoric made up of invention, style and arrangement can exist in a vacuum, she says; it is memory and delivery that connect it to "history, culture, and the life of the polis" ("Platonic" 9).

Welch says that the importance of memory is apparent in the phrase we use for memorization *by heart.* "Remembering something, carrying something around with oneself, takes place at the center of one's being" ("Platonic" 7; *Contemporary* 98). It also takes us out of our isolated selves, binding us to a larger sense of reality: "Memory is also the existence of the past within the present. It is there that culture and rhetoric largely exist, for Plato and for us" (*Contemporary* 98). In *The Contemporary Reception of Classical Rhetoric*, Welch says that a "major problem with the truncated canons and an overemphasis on the text lies in the fact that they do not have any aim. They lose meaning because they are prevented, by the deletion of memory and delivery, from referring to any life outside the text" (131). For Plato, Welch says,

> Memory is an inclusive system of mind and soul that transcends the individual person's ability to encompass it and that at the same time offers that individual a way to realize his or her capacities more fully; that is, memory enables an individual to achieve his or her *arete*, or unique excellence. (130)

Welch hits squarely the crucial argument for reconsidering memory. Rhetoric is a cultural and a psychological phenomenon. The past is carried in the present not just individually; rhetoric is a collective unconscious, a means of making and retrieving memories. The "psychology of discourse" ("Platonic" 10; *Contemporary* 101) is what Welch calls Plato's use of the canon of memory. Discourse, or dialectic, depends on the mutual understanding that memory creates.

Welch's works connect this last idea with the "secondary orality" (Walter Ong's term for the world of electronic media) of the present technological era, too. Like Covino, she stresses that language prescribes thought; our possibilities for expanded or limited thought are determined by the language we use. New forms of language can create new ways of thinking. Today, our ways of thinking are changed by the secondarily oral world of electronic media (see Welch's "Electrifying Classical Rhetoric: Ancient Media, Modern Technology, and Contemporary Composition"). Welch maintains throughout her work that memory remains important in written discourse but is crucial in a time of electronic, secondarily oral discourse, for our memories will now contain *memoria* in another form. The new discourse combines the written and the oral and demands an understanding of how both modes of discourse work. "At issue," Welch says, "is the shaping of consciousness from which all encoding derives. ... We must face the interiorization of electronic media as Plato in his rhetoric faced the interiorization of the phonetic alphabet" ("Electrifying" 14–15). Clearly, a revised concept of memory aids our comprehension of the new discourse.

Welch's work is informed by the earlier works of Walter Ong and Marshall McLuhan, which describe changes created by mass media and technology. According to Ong, the secondary orality that mass media and technology bring us does appeal to enormous audiences. Unlike primary orality, which preceded print, secondary orality depends on print. Though it seems spontaneous, it is not; it has been produced with care and with written scripts (*Orality* 135–138). And its effect is far-reaching. McLuhan suggests in *Understanding Media* that through the mass media it may be possible "to by-pass languages in favor of a general cosmic consciousness which might be very like the collective unconscious" (84). Patrick Mahony's 1969 essay on McLuhan and rhetoric notes that although McLuhan's emphasis is on the delivery (the medium is the message), delivery is closely allied with memory: "memory or information storage has been exteriorized into new media or forms of pronunciation" (14). Mahony cites Kenneth Burke's statement that whereas classical rhetoric stressed persuasion, new rhetoric stresses identification, "which can be a partially 'unconscious' factor in its appeal" (15). If Burke is correct, then the human desire to identify gives mass media an edge in convincing its audiences. Thus we have a new kind of rhetoric through which huge numbers of people find commonality by internalizing *en masse* new structures and new experiences. This phenomenon is discussed as well in chapter 7 in reference to the books by Hardison and Bolter: Old concepts "disappear" and new ones restructure our thinking.

Frederick Reynolds' articles "Concepts of Memory in Contemporary Composition" and "Memory Issues in Composition Studies" address these issues. In "Concepts of Memory" Reynolds cites Mahony as an early voice in rhetoric and composition for acknowledging memory's many and vital roles in writing. Reynolds points out four ways that modern composition studies have been treating memory. First, memory is mnemonics: Students are taught to scan readings by sight, looking for information (e.g., in headings or topic sentences) that will help them remember or find what they need to know.

Second, writing teachers and texts teach how to make writing memorable. Reynolds notes the *St. Martin's Guide to Writing* as an example of textbook treatments of this. Chapters 2 and 3 are entitled "Remembering People" and "Remembering Events." Each chapter, when suggesting a different type of writing, includes a section called "Invention and Research" which includes searching in memory for ideas. A chapter called "Invention and Inquiry" emphasizes prewriting techniques; the chapter "Cueing the Reader" discusses conventions that meet readers' expectations. Reynolds says that books like this one have "imbedded throughout … an implicit notion of memory as the development of memorable subjects, words, phrases, sentences, passages and texts. Similarly imbedded is a notion of memory as a set of information repositories to be tapped" ("Concepts" 249). Reynolds looked at the second edition; the third and fourth editions are similar.

Third, tapping these memory repositories is examined. Reynolds uses the classical distinction between natural and artificial memory, suggesting that the natural memory works narratively and the artificial analytically. He also differentiates between short- and long-term memory. Short term contains information that guides style; long term expresses ideas and structure. He cites Flower and Hayes, among others, as researchers who have expanded our understanding of the connections between memory and the composing process.

Fourth, composition and memory are linked through psychology, and Reynolds uses examples from Welch, Flower and Hayes, and others to argue that understanding the link between writing and psychology is important and that memory offers us the key to this study.

Frederick Reynolds' 1993 collection *Rhetorical Memory and Delivery: Classical Concepts for Contemporary Composition and Communication* covers a broad range of the issues that surface as we reconsider the forgotten canons. Many of the book's contributors are cited in these pages. The important feature throughout the book is the consideration of the critical changes in our memory systems that occur with electronic delivery. Winifred Bryan Horner sums up the issues the book addresses in her introduction by suggesting that the new electronic delivery systems create a communal memory that affects us intellectually and socially. We must look carefully, she states, at the effect of this memory on invention, on literature, on our epistemologies, and on our thought processes (xi).

An interesting connection between memory and style is made by Rick Cypert in "A Return to the Treasure-House of Invention: Memory in the Composition Classroom." Cypert suggests that, just as language creates meaning, language also calls up and transforms memory into appropriate discourse for the particular rhetorical situation. In other words, thinking about *how* to say something is what brings that something into consciousness. Cypert says, "While style is related to the *product* of Invention, it seems to me that it also may aid the *process* in a way we don't often think about: [as] an agent and inducer of memory, a friend to our cognitive schemata, a way toward the commonplaces that for our students may not be so common anymore" (37).

Cypert notes the dialectical nature of memory and writing. When the language we use pleases us, Cypert believes, that language prompts us to further thought and invention. Thus just as memory helps us write, writing helps us to remember: "I don't know what I know until I have retrieved this image by transforming it into language; nor can I share it with others" (37). In "Memory: A Step Toward Invention," he suggests that in the writing classroom we need to call forth memories intentionally and to study how they come, to study strategies for getting them and then to place them "into particular contexts, building rhetorical worlds for them to live in" ("Memory" 3). This is a worthy exercise because "our memory serves as our *pistis* or proof for every thought or utterance we make" (3). If memory generates thought, we can expand our thinking by learning how to expand the use of memory.

In *The Methodical Memory: Invention in Current-Traditional Rhetoric*, Sharon Crowley discusses what is wrong with current-traditional rhetoric. Crowley describes a tradition that begins with George Campbell and continues even today, a tradition emphasizing that the memory works in an organized fashion and is an accurate representation of past experience, so much so that even an outline jogs the memory by representing the ways that information had been stored. Crowley explains the legacy of current-traditional rhetoric this way:

> Invention consisted in the rhetor's retrospective review of her ideas and the connections made between them; arrangement consisted in composing a discourse where the ordering of parts exactly reflected whatever mental processes had been followed in reaching conclusions. (*Methodical* 45)

The result of this emphasis on the organizational capacity of memory is that it "removed invention from the chronology of memory and relocated it within the spatial interstices of the outline" (*Methodical* 99). Any thought of memory or invention as natural processes is ignored.

This theory of "introspective invention" assumes that memory is methodical and that it will "record and faithfully repeat a process of investigation" (*Methodical* 23). It assumes, too, that people have this gift of memory in varying degrees, and that only those with a highly developed methodical memory will have anything to say worth reading. These assumptions make life hard for the new freshman student, who may have had little experience with the world and therefore would have little to say (especially when it must all be put in third person, rendering the most personal memories generic). Regarding the memory as only an individual, organized storehouse, Crowley says, results in low expectations of student writing in current-traditional classrooms. The blame for the poor writing was put not on the model of invention, but on the deficient memories of the students (*Methodical* 90).

What the student must remember, then, is form, which, Crowley suggests, creates what Jasper Neel calls "antiwriting": "student texts simply announce that their authors are observing the syntactic and organizational rules they have been taught to follow" (*Teacher's* 45). This writing is "thoroughly technologized, pure ritual" (45). It is "almost wholly reliant on a writer's ability to perform a carefully prescribed set of mental gymnastics" (*Methodical* 68).

Two big considerations are missing in current-traditional practices. One is the constructive, inventive power of the writing act itself. Instead of using writing to provoke thought, current-traditional rhetoric locates both memory and invention in "an isolated mental region … ideally prior to, and separate from, engagement with language" (*Methodical* 68). The other missing consideration is the culture in which the writing student is immersed.

Current-traditionalists turned memory back into memorization, favoring arrangement and style. The filing cabinet of the mind became filled with prescriptive forms. Memorizing the prescriptive forms gave one the paraphernalia to write well and achieve appropriate "socialization" (*Methodical* 137), as Crowley calls it. She illustrates the antiwriting these practices create in her example of a perfectly organized five-paragraph theme. It begins "X is one of the most important problems in today's modern society. There are three main reasons why X should be stopped …" (*Methodical* 149). Memorization is at work here. Natural memory and invention are not. Nor is any sense of engagement between the writer and either his text or his reader. Nor is the possibility of "differance." Current-traditional rhetoric at its worst has taken all the joy out of writing and reading because it has taken away any possibility of reconstruction or invention on the part of the writer or the reader. Although the word *memory* is not often one she uses, Ann Berthoff treats issues of memory throughout her work. In "Rhetoric as Hermeneutic," she clarifies the connection between self and society. She sees human beings as neither isolated individuals nor completely social beings, but as a combination of the two. Interpretation, she says, is necessarily social: "We live not in Nature alone, but in History and Culture, in a world built by language" (284). At the same time, "we aren't born in groups" (285–286). Our experiences, albeit social, are never just like another's experiences. If we are to reclaim rhetoric as a "hermeneutic enterprise" (281), one based on interpretation, we must allow for a dialectic between "the private and the public" (286):

> Language ... [is] an instrumentality: it is the instrument of one's becoming, at once, one's self and representative of humanity. ... It is as historical creatures that we have the power of choice; language—the means of naming and re-naming, or representing and articulating the options—provides the saving image of transformation. Consciousness of the power of language liberates the imagination, the active mind with its power of memory and envisagement. For *power*, read *freedom*; read *life*. (286)

We have to acknowledge a combination of social and personal forces, combined through "the power of memory and envisagement," the key to imagination.

Berthoff says, "Students can learn to write by learning the uses of chaos, which is to say, by rediscovering the power of language to generate meanings" (*Making* 39). Here she's addressing what is disorganized in, hidden in, or missing from memory. For instance, she says that we must teach students "to tolerate ambiguity and be patient with their beginnings" (39). She suggests that *meaning* is created by addressing, by playing with, the imperfect memory (and addressing it is an act of imagination). The imagination brings symbolic forms to consciousness through "memory and the power of envisagement" (92). Thus writing becomes a meaning-making activity as language, imagination, and memory join to produce and clarify relationships.

When Berthoff talks about reclaiming the imagination, she is talking about an act that involves memory, too:

> looking—and looking again—engages the mind, and until that happens, no authentic composing is going to take place. ... When Coleridge spoke of imagination, he meant both "the Prime agent of all human perception" and the shaping power, that "all-in-each" of every mind as it gives form to thought and feeling. Both visual images—percepts—and the "mental" images we call up from memory, or which we invent, are representative of the forms of understanding; thus we say, "I *see* what you *mean*." (*Reclaiming* 3)

Memory is part of "looking again" (as we remember and compare the first look), it is the "all-in-each" in the mind, and it is the storehouse of images which allow us to understand. Memory helps us to reclaim the imagination.

Modern rhetoricians, thus, are taking memory seriously again, perhaps for the first time since classical times and certainly for the first time since the advent of the modern age (Sharon Crowley dates the beginning of the modern age with the work of John Locke ["Modern" 32]). Important in all of their work is the emphasis on the generative nature of memory. It is this view of memory as a creator of knowledge, as a precursor to or a part of invention, that justifies studying memory in composition and rhetoric. Just as psychological and scientific interest in memory has burgeoned because of new research, rhetorical interest in the lost canons of memory and delivery will continue to grow as we learn more about the way the mind works and as technology changes our methods of communication.

Memory and Composition Theory

From its beginning, modern composition theory has validated memory as a generative force. As early as 1964, Janet Emig acknowledged the importance of the unconscious, or perhaps the preconscious, as she calls it in an introductory dialogue to "The Uses of the Unconscious in Composing." She encourages going with your daemon, having habits that work for you. Freshmen students' texts, on the other hand, are so often conscious: They seem "to have been written from one layer of the self—the ectoderm only, with student involvement in his own thought and language moving down an unhappy scale from sporadic engagement to abject diffidence" (*Web* 46). She notes in "The Composing Processes of Twelfth Graders" that habits which suggest using memory—stopping, engaging in digressions, contemplating, and reformulating—are seldom done in school-sponsored writing. In school, memory is mainly used for remembering a "set of stylistic principles" probably set out by the teacher (*Web* 90). Writing that brings memory into play (writing which is created through recursive practices) is more likely to be done in self-sponsored writing outside of the classroom.

Memory plays the crucial role in the cognitive composition theory of Linda Flower and John Hayes, whose work stems from research in cognitive psychology (see chapter 3). They divide writing into three major elements—the task environment, the writer's long-term memory, and the writing process itself. Flower and Hayes describe long-term memory as:

a storehouse of knowledge about the topic and audience, as well as knowledge of writing plans and problem representations. Sometimes a single cue in an assignment … can let a writer tap a stored representation of a problem and bring a whole raft of writing plans into play. ("Cognitive" 371)

Flower later extended the definition of what is in long-term memory to include "the writer's assumptions," "prior knowledge," and "the political, economic, and historical forces that could be said to write the writer" ("Cognition, Context, and Theory Building" 284), acknowledging more particularly the large body of information and experience stored in memory. Long-term memory is a large, relatively stable repository. It stores ideas in many different ways, both verbal and nonverbal.

However, it is in the short-term memory that the stored ideas—images, schema, abstractions, and so on—get translated into text. This is the "working memory"; its job is "the creation and the translation of ... alternative mental representations of meaning" ("Images" 122). Flower and Hayes suggest from their protocol analyses that writers are constantly translating and revising as they write, testing their ideas against the representations in long-term memory and reformulating them in short-term memory. Thus both parts of memory, working together, are crucial to the composing process.

In "The Cognition of Discovery: Defining a Rhetorical Problem," Flower and Hayes discuss the difference between expert and novice writers as they approach a writing task. Expert writers have more "stored plans" to help them figure out how to write their papers. These plans include conventions as well as a feel for appropriate tone and phrases (29). Novice writers, on the other hand, go to their memories for their own experiences rather than for strategies that might help them write to an audience. Obviously, the more stored plans a writer has in memory, the easier it is to find an appropriate one for the writing task at hand. The conventions suggested or dictated by those plans eliminate many decisions about the writing task.

Discovery, then, involves searching in long-term memory for possible strategies and using short-term memory to combine and redesign those choices into an appropriate strategy for the task at hand. Flower and Hayes conclude that discovery is not magical but is teachable: We can teach our students to "create inspiration" by teaching them "to explore and define their own problems, even within the constraints of an assignment" ("Cognition of Discovery" 32). We do this by teaching them to use the interplay of long- and short-term memory.

Similarly, Stephen Witte recognizes the importance of memory with his concept of *pretext*—a "writer's tentative linguistic representation of intended meaning, a 'trial locution' that is produced in the mind, stored in the writer's memory, and sometimes manipulated mentally prior to being transcribed as written text" (397). Citing the work of Flower and Hayes and Bareiter and Scardamalia, Witte contends that writers hold pretexts in memory and revise those even before producing written text. Witte urges that more study be done on the revision processes of writers, and that the study include the revision of pretext, that which is held in memory and never written down. It has significant influence on the written words finally chosen. The concept of pretext suggests that it is memory which creates and evaluates these trial-and-error locutions before they are put to paper or even consciously examined.

Sondra Perl offers a different description of the ideas, perceptions, and words that fill the memory. Perl documents three recursive features of composing: rereading bits of discourse, returning to the topic idea, and returning "to feelings of non-verbalized perceptions that *surround* the words, or to what the words already present evoke in the reader. ... The move occurs inside the writer, to what is physically felt" (114). This she calls the "felt sense," using philosopher Eugene Gendlin's term.

He defines it as

> the soft underbelly of thought ... a bodily awareness that ... encompasses everything you feel and know about a given subject at a given time. ... It is body and mind before they are split apart. (qtd. in Perl 115)

Perl thinks the felt sense may be the same as "inner voice" or "inspiration." Working with the felt sense allows us to write "something new and fresh." We "attend" the felt sense: "there is less 'figuring out' an answer and more 'waiting' to see what forms" (116).

Perl calls this "attending" retrospective structuring: "It is retrospective in that it begins with what is already there, inchoately, and brings whatever is there forward by using language in structured form" (117). The process leads to freshness, discovery, and surprise—all made possible through memory. Perl's retrospective structuring is joined with what she calls *projective structuring,* which is the crafting of ideas so that they are intelligible to an audience. The shuttling back and forth between retrospective and projective structuring creates a nice dialectic between self and audience. Unfortunately, Perl says, many writers are impatient with the retrospective structuring, and they make projective structuring a rules-oriented activity. Her complaint echoes Emig's comment that students often ignore the pausing/restructuring/recollecting parts of the process while doing school-sponsored writing. Teachers need to allow time for these forays into memory if students are to understand their value and write "by heart."

A similar idea about the process of generating text comes from James Britton; his term is "shaping at the point of utterance." Britton says that by reading and being read to, we can internalize forms and rhythms of the written language which we then have to draw upon when it is time to write (18): We have these concepts of language in our memory. Writing, he says, begins by "drawing upon interpreted experience" and even "a mere apperception of the felt quality of 'experiencing'" (17). Thus writing is a contemplative act, one in which the writing itself prompts invention; writing is "hearing an inner voice dictating forms of the written language appropriate to the task at hand" (18). The inner voice is based on memory, on the speaking, listening, and reading experiences the writer has had.

Alice Brand, in her article "The Why of Cognition: Emotion and the Writing Process," underscores the importance of memory in the psychology of writing, especially writer's block and apprehension. She says that the profession itself doesn't acknowledge how important memory is to cognition, that "it suffers a blind spot when it explains how long-term memory and language interact" (437). We never can have all of what is in memory at our beck and call; we choose. "Writing, too, is an exercise in inclusion and exclusion, a lesson in decision making and choice," Brand says (437). She believes that those choices are made for affective or emotional reasons and that those choices determine writing style.

The connections between writing and reading become clearer as we use memory to describe them. Reading theorist Frank Smith calls our long-term memory "our permanent source of understanding of the world" (*Understanding* 6). He explains that good readers use memory constantly to understand the letters and words on the page: They select, they chunk (organize elements—like letters—into meaningful units—like words), they predict. Selection, chunking, and prediction are feats of memory, successfully done when there is more "prior knowledge" to aid the process. Memory provides strategies for reading just as it does for writing. (See Robert J. Tierney and P. David Pearson's "Toward a Composing Model of Reading" for an informative comparison of the two interactive processes.)

In *Joining the Literacy Club*, Smith examines the connection between memory and learning, and his comments are apt:

> Memory is a part of all learning, perception, and thinking, inevitably and usually unconsciously. (117)

> We learn most easily when something is relevant, when it is useful, makes sense, and we have no fear of failing to learn. And we remember most easily when what we need to recall is most relevant and useful, and we have no anxiety about not remembering. (117)

> the most deliberate and contrived efforts to manipulate memory occur when the control is in the hands of someone else—when we are told to bring something to mind. The worst conditions for memory, like the worst conditions for learning, are when someone tells us precisely what we should be doing. (118)

> Situations in which we are engaged invoke the memories that come to mind for us. Learning and remembering are both social events. (119)

Notice how easy it is to substitute "writing" for "learning" in these quotes.

Smith believes that education has "backed the wrong horse" by following psychology, particularly as it concerns itself with learning theory, for it studies the *forced* memory: that which can be remembered when we are told what to recall. Remembering is suddenly considered difficult. Anthropology, on the other hand, studies the natural memory, which works quite effortlessly when what we need to remember is relevant and useful (*Joining* 117–118). (The anthropological methods are employed in recent natural memory studies, which represent a reaction within psychology against just what Smith criticizes.)

Time, silence, delay—these are factors that Donald Murray says a writer needs to write the unexpected. Writing cannot be forced; it must be given the opportunity to come forth. The essays in *Expecting the Unexpected* suggest a process like Perl, Witte, and Britton describe:

> Students need a problem to solve—a meaning they need to make—and the space in which *not* to write about it. Time for staring out the window, daydreaming, thinking and not thinking, allowing the brain to collect and connect, fitting and discarding fragments of information that may construct meaning—and may not. (111)

Surprise is Murray's term for unexpectedly fresh, new writing, and he believes that students create surprising writing by experiencing the process of discovering themselves. *Musing* seems a good term for what he recommends, giving the memory free play to generate both words and ideas.

All composition theory that promotes freewriting, like Peter Elbow's ideas put forth in *Writing Without Teachers* and Toby Fulwiler's in *The Journal Book*, accepts memory as an important generative force. Freewriting allows the memory to be emptied on the page, regardless of the value of its contents; it is the dumping itself that is of value. Journals are most often spiral-bound freewriting. Freewriting or journal writing allows students to "wonder aloud" (Fulwiler 3), synthesize, digress, revise—all mental acts that involve the memory.

Prewriting strategies engage memory as well. Richard Young commends prewriting as an activity that stimulates our memory for both ideas and forms; memory helps us discover what we know. Young's concerns with methods of discovery and invention are primarily to help the writer with retrieval of what is already known: We must "develop the creative potential of the writer in dealing with his or her own experience" (37). Otherwise (and here Young quotes Gordon Rohman, who first advanced prewriting in the 1960s), "to continue to teach rhetoric without attention to discovery reinforces that indifference to meaning that characterizes the modern world of politics and advertising" (33; Rohman 112). A 1991 study by W. Michael Reed and Thomas M. Sherman shows differences between honors students and basic writers in how they value and utilize prewriting strategies. They determined that honors students wrote their best essays when they both used a prewriting heuristic and wrote down their ideas. Basic writers did best when they did neither, and did worst when they used a heuristic but wrote nothing down. Reed and Sherman conclude that:

> because basic writers have not developed writing habits that include cognitive strategies to generate and store ideas as part of their prewriting repertoire, they may need extensive instruction and experience in order to employ them effectively. (76)

By increasing their strategies for using memory during prewriting, basic writers may increase the complexity of their writing.

Jeannette Harris stresses prewriting while stating that discovery occurs throughout the composing process, even in revision, when the writer is still "retrieving additional information, making further connections, recognizing emerging patterns" (15). In prewriting as well as free-writing and keeping journals, ideas and forms are discovered by provoking memory. In addition, the personal nature of much prewriting and freewriting serve as an affirmation that the memory of the student writer has a valid place in the writing classroom.

Memory serves writers in another way. In "Why Write?" Richard Young and Patricia Sullivan suggest that writers can hold in short-term memory the relatively simple structures for writing narrative or descriptive works. But analytic/synthetic writing tasks are much more difficult, and it is the writing itself that helps probe the long-term and organize the short-term memory. Writing is then "epistemic" (222); writing is thinking. Young and Sullivan suggest that part of students' success or failure at complex writing might be a question of memory management. They conclude with this suggestion:

The relationship between memory and the activity of writing suggests the possibility of a modern art of memory, roughly analogous to the classical art but focusing on the interaction of writing and memory at the point of utterance. ... A modern art of memory might provide explicit strategies for increasing the power of short-term memory and for accessing long-term memory more effectively. But a "modern art of memory" might be only another name for an art of invention approached from a new and interesting direction. (225)

They suggest seeing memory/invention not just as the task of retrieval from long-term memory, but as a collection of strategies for "combining smaller units of thought and discourse into larger units" and strategies for "suppressing stereotypic responses" that may be stored in memory (225). Their theory enlarges memory functions for writing and suggests that memory management can help us not only in our personal writing tasks but in the way we see our culture. Managing memory gives us the opportunity for re-vision, for looking at ourselves and the world around us from a fresh point of view.

This connection between memory, invention, and culture is supported by Karen Burke LeFevre in *Invention as a Social Act*. The Platonic idea of invention assumed "individual introspection: ideas are created in the mind of an atomistic individual and then expressed to the rest of the world" (LeFevre 1). LeFevre refutes this view of invention; she contends that invention is social in nature rather than private. Whether working singly or collaboratively, authors are never completely removed from the language, attitudes, and conventions of their culture.

LeFevre's concept of *invention* includes memory. She regards invention in four ways, each of which incorporates memory. First, invention is "active creating—as well as finding or remembering—that which is the substance of discourse" (46): Remembering is part of the creative act. Second, it involves "a variety of social relationships" (46): This takes place as writers work with others, tapping other memories to enrich their own. Third, it is "a dialectical process in which individuals interact with socioculture" (46): They work within the language and conventions of their "socioculture," which determines the makeup of memory. Fourth, invention is "brought to completion by an audience, often extending over time" (47): Writing is made memorable; it is interpreted by other beings with other memories and incorporated into their stores of experience. Just as LeFevre studies "the individual inventor ... through the lens of a social perspective" (127), we too can look at the individual memory through that same lens. We can bring the art of memory back into the classroom, giving students a chance to use all that they know.

Scholars and teachers of rhetoric and composition believe that memory is an important part of the creative process. In the many ways already represented, they are making a strong case for actively teaching strategies for putting memory to work. As the preceding survey shows, memory is alive and well in rhetoric and composition. The field of composition studies has been categorized in different ways—Stephen North breaks it into practitioners, scholars, and researchers; Lester Faigley and James Berlin divide its members according to their philosophical views—expressive, cognitive, and social. Interest in memory is found in all these categories. The study of memory and its place in the writing process transcends the differences reflected by the categories, just as the study of memory and its place in the thinking process transcends the boundaries of disciplines.

Implications for Teaching

It is a big step from the current-traditional vision of rhetoric as a combination of invention, arrangement, and style to a vision of rhetoric that generates from the memory of the individual-in-a-culture. Yet taking that step is a way to break out of the limited view of rhetoric that has been the mainstay of composition teaching for over 100 years. Now we are challenged to devise strategies for teaching students how to cultivate the resources of memory. Although the purpose of this book is not to serve as a pedagogical guide for involving memory in the writing process, let me note some pedagogical possibilities suggested by the information collected here.

Predominant among the suggested practices is teaching writing as a process. Obviously, parts of the process (like prewriting) foster memory, and so does the recursive nature of the whole process itself: Recollection, review, and revision are acts of memory. Another message is that writing takes *time*—to write, to reflect, to muse. Time allows us to put the memory into gear and "find" in our experience what we want to say. We must encourage our students to take this time—perhaps by providing it in the classroom—and we can help them understand that musing is a productive act. As Ann Berthoff says, we can help them to learn the uses of chaos (*Making*). We should foster ungraded and unfinished writing (e.g., freewriting, journals, drafts) to promote comfort with the act of writing and to allow more opportunity to "wonder" (Covino). It narrows the gap between the kind of self-sponsored writing that is met with reflection and the kind of school-sponsored writing that usually is not.

We can promote memory through personal writing. Kathleen Welch advocates autobiographical writing; she says that it gives authority (of one's own life and experience) as well as identity (with one's own culture) ("Autobiography" 6). Robert Connors advocates personal writing for those same reasons: It is an essential step toward joining the conversation of the university. He observes that an 18-year-old student lacks the experience (i.e., store of memories) to speak comfortably on many subjects. It may be, however, that the student only lacks skill at academic discourse. Terry Myers Zawacki argues for the personal essay in order to "privilege other ways of knowing and representing the world" than just the critical essay, which promotes thinking in terms of authority, hierarchy, and competition (34). She believes that the personal essay allows for other ways of "knowing," ways suggested by Belenky, Clinchy, Goldberger, and Tarule in *Women's Ways of Knowing* (33). Joel Haefner uses the personal essay to "remind" writers of the cultural and social forces behind writing.

Rick Cypert assigns two people to remember and write about the same event and then compare their stories. He says that the comparison reveals "a great deal

... about the nature of truth, the difficulty in constructing a clear-cut, infallible argument, and the necessity of fluency in language to discover what one knows (and does not know) and to communicate both the breadth and limitations of that knowledge ("Memory" 5).

Jim Corder says that teachers must ask the following questions about their student writers:

> What is it we expect them to remember?
> Do they know that they need to remember?
> Do they know recipes?
> Do they know—do we provide or show—ways of thought,
> available patterns, structures?
> Do they know and remember habituations of writing?
> Do they own information? (12)

He concludes unhappily that the writing done in composition classes usually "ignores the need for remembered information, method and insight" (12).

Corder suggests that we should ask these questions *about* our writing students. I think we should ask them *of* our students and *of* ourselves as well, over and over.

Current textbooks really don't emphasize memory at all. Most textbooks reflect the practices and preferences of traditional invention-arrangement-style writing teachers rather than new composition theory. They may have a section on personal, autobiographical writing, but little else. John Frederick Reynolds' description of *The St. Martin's Guide to Writing* exemplifies how textbooks deal with memory in a round-about way.

Still, there are textbooks that recognize memory's improving status. James Moffett's *Active Voices* is broken up into four processes: recollection, investigation, imagination, and cogitation. Obviously recollection—autobiography and memoir—deals with memory, as recollecting is probing the memory to remember the past. But for Moffett, imagination and cogitation involve memory, too, as these processes "create second-order experiences of the mind. ... we recombine and transform first- and secondhand experiences" (iii). Although he does not emphasize memory per se as the generator of these processes, his suggestions and assignments reflect the importance of recollecting and reorganizing experience to be expressed in more sophisticated written forms.

Eve Shelnutt's book, *Writing: The Translation of Memory*, is a reader filled with student texts, chiefly short stories and expository essays. Shelnutt says that teaching her first writing courses made her believe that:

> what the students failed to honor was their memories and the *distance* that memory provides. A person in the act of remembering is in two places at once: in the real place and time of the present and in the place and time recollected. The difference between the times and places produces a heightened awareness within the individual remembering; and from that awareness, a perspective emerges, a new way of seeing. (iii)

Shelnutt believes that students see all writing as *fictions*, "the conscious choice and arrangement of content creates an invention that is not so much factual as suggestive of the truth" (iv). Her books gives drafts of each work and the writer's comments. Her approach brings memory (as a strategic device for writing) and memories (as inspiration) to the forefront of the students' minds as they begin to write by showing them how much is in memory and how thinking about memories helps shape them into writing.

Two textbooks that are notable for their attention to memory are Winifred Bryan Horner's *Rhetoric in the Classical Tradition* and Sharon Crowley's *Ancient Rhetorics for Contemporary Students*. Both are based on classical principles, and both are organized according to the five original canons of rhetoric rather than the more typical truncation to three canons.

Horner's book allots memory a full 40 pages. She explains the chapter this way:

> Where classical rhetoric limited the study of memory to cultivating the natural memory, modern rhetoric must consider memory in terms of the resources available through books and databases. Therefore the following chapter will consider two kinds of memory: the cultural memory and the individual memory. As the classical rhetoricians devised ways to store and retrieve information from the human memory, the modern rhetorician must also consider ways to retrieve information from books, libraries, and computers. (339)

Horner's book has been praised by reviewers, whose comments show the regard given to her chapter on memory. Richard Enos notes that the she binds memory to creativity and that she sees access to information as the basis for invention (170). Frederick Reynolds praises her attention to cultural memory. He also applauds the reinstitution of memory and delivery into the teaching of rhetoric, for, he says, "the reduction [to three canons] destroys the system; it removes rhetoric's context and power, and robs the canons of their completeness and connectedness. Second, the reduction perpetuates itself" ("Redefining" 202).

Our textbooks have a long way to go before they give memory adequate treatment in rhetoric and in the composing process. But at least the interest is growing. The approaches to memory taken by researchers in composition are admittedly different from one another. In common, though, they all recognize and affirm memory as a powerful creative tool. In different ways, they illuminate the role memory plays in the thinking/writing process.

We must find more ways to help students probe and appreciate their own memories. This means going beyond the work done so far in composition theory. It means taking what we can learn from philosophy, psychology, and literature. It means examining the assumptions we bring to writing, for our cultural training has loaded our memories with the belief that writing should be done, or should look, a certain way. It means understanding from whence those expectations come, and resisting them when we feel they do not work for us. When we address memory thus at the beginning of the composing process, writing is connected with our lives, our language, and our thoughts; it is no longer a separate skill. We empower our students with more knowledge and the authority to use it.

If we teach our students to search, use, and value their own memories when they write, we foster rhetoric that breaks out of the chains of standardized thinking and writing. We accept and enjoy "differance"; we allow room for alternative rhetorics, for a multiplicity or carnival of voices. We can then write more truly, read more critically, and listen more acutely.

Chapter 7

Re/Membering Culture(s)

Musing

Several weeks ago, I read in the local newspaper about a half-day seminar called "Improving Your Memory." It was to be put on by the hospital's community education department, and it targeted senior citizens. Nevertheless, I decided to go, partly because of my interest in memory in general and partly because of my specific concern about the seemingly early demise of my own. I waited till the day before to call for a reservation.

"Oh, honey, you can't get a reservation now," the bemused volunteer at the other end of the phone told me. "This topic's always booked up way in advance!"

The more I learn about memory, the more I know that I don't want my own to go.

I have just finished reading Barbara Kingsolver's Animal Dreams for the second time. It's about Codi, a woman in her 30s who goes back to the small Arizona town she grew up in. The name of the town, ironically, is Grace. She goes back for two reasons. One is be near her father, who was once the town doctor but now suffers from Alzheimer's disease. I think it was partly the portrayal of her father that made me try to sign up for the memory seminar. The other reason she goes back is to try to make some sense out of her life by revisiting the place of her past. She goes back to her father because he's lost his memory and to her childhood home because she needs to find hers.

The plot is complicated by the entrance of her old boyfriend, Loyd, an Apache whose reverence for memory and memories is rooted deep in his culture. He helps Codi face her own past, but more than that, he teaches her the value of those memories. She tries to leave again, but she can't; her transformation is one that leads her right back to Grace. She learns what he seems to know instinctively—that memories are our most valuable possession.

The book ends with Codi remembering for the first time that she was present on the day of her mother's death.

"You remember that?" said Viola, the woman with her.

"I thought I did. But people told me I hadn't, so I'd about decided I'd made it up."

"No, if you remember something, then it's true," Viola told her. "In the long run, that's what you've got."

In the long run, that's what I've got. Not a life full of moments lived but a head full of the memories of those moments. And I keep watching for another memory seminar. When it comes around again, I'll get my reservation in early.

* * *

Blizzards of paper
in slow motion
sift through her.
In nightmares she suddenly recalls
a class she signed up for
but forgot to attend.
Now it is too late.
Now it is time for finals;
losers will be shot.
Phrases of men who lectured her
drift and rustle in piles:
Why don't you speak up?
Why are you shouting?
You have the wrong answer,
wrong line, wrong face.
They tell her she is the womb-man,
babymachine, mirror image, toy,
earth mother and penis-poor,
a dish of synthetic strawberry icecream
rapidly melting.
She grunts to a halt.
She must learn again to speak
starting with I
starting with We
starting as the infant does
with her own true hunger
and pleasure
and rage.

("Unlearning Not to Speak" by Marge Piercy)

Art and Culture in the 20th Century

Alienation defines our modern culture. Before the 20th century, it was easy for people to consider themselves linked with their heritage; they saw evidence of it every day. Today, our connections with the past are ever fewer. The implications of this are enormous, including a basically new way of looking at man, at the earth, and at machines.

World War I probably changed the Western world more than any historical event. World War II, coming so soon after, widened the gulf between us and our history, perhaps making it impassable. The experience of the wars, combined with the industrial and then technological revolutions, has changed our identities, and we no longer feel linked to history and tradition. Artistically, scientifically, socially, and politically, this has been a century of change and of revolution. Nowhere has this been more apparent than in the arts. The 20th century has staged a revolt—brash, ugly, anti-"ideal," stripped of preconceptions—literally divorced from history. To borrow Rorty's term, the 20th-century arts speak in a sometimes frightfully abnormal discourse as they search for ways to express their dissociation with the past.

Disappearing Through the Skylight: Culture and Technology in the Twentieth Century by O. B. Hardison is an interesting analysis of modern art within the framework of modern culture. I emphasize Hardison's work here because it describes a social phenomenon moving in a direction similar to the dialogue of many contemporary thinkers.

Hardison's account of the arts today shows us a rejection of the past. Examples of this rejection abound in architecture, art, music, and poetry, and Hardison sees technology as inevitably fostering the rejection. With possibilities never before imagined, the arts will never again be the same. Art has rejected history partly as a reaction to its sense of alienation from the past (e.g., "I no longer belong to that tradition"). It turns not only from history, but also to the present and future because it has possibilities never before imagined (e.g., "I have all sorts of new art to create." Hardison believes that "[t]o reject history is to move in the direction of abstraction" (85). Symbols are "detached from their contexts," "liberated from history"; "they become designs" (86). This creates a mental desert he calls "an Arizona of the mind" (86). He uses as an example the International Style in architecture, which designed structures that were geometric, huge, abstract, and universal, without a sense of a history. Compare that style, Hardison suggests, with the architecture of the U.S. Capital, which is loaded with historical meaning, which makes us "remember" whole concepts of government and civilization that the architecture represents. This meaning, the re-presentation, is absent in modern art. For instance, the Dada art movement of the early 20th century professed to mean nothing: "It is an art, rather, of images without content and words without meaning" (168). And Hardison discusses similar change in poetry and music. Italian poet Eugenio Montale, in "The Second Life of Art," mourns the loss of connection in modern art primarily because the art "denies itself its second and larger life: the life of memory and everyday circulation" (21):

music, painting, and poetry begin to be understood when they are presented but they do not truly live if they lack the capacity to continue to exercise their powers beyond the moment, freeing themselves, mirroring themselves in that particular situation of life which made them possible. (22)

Memory, he is saying, is what brings art alive. (Art, on the other hand, may bring memory alive, too. For an interesting account of the connection between memory and visual art and of the cultural implications of that connection, see Susanne Kuchler & Walter Melion, *Images of Memory: On Remembering and Representation*.)

Hardison is saying that the 20th century is an age of forgetting. It is an age where, on one hand, remembering the past seems unnecessary because the past seems irrelevant. On the other hand, though, the lack of connection with the past causes alienation, the epidemic of our late 20th-century society. Alienation is a hazard associated with detachment from the past.

Technology and Forgetting

Perhaps the most interesting way in which modern art casts off the past is in its celebration of technology. Technology offers a completely new present and an exciting future to the arts in ways which seem to have nothing to do with the past. Perhaps memory can even serve us poorly in a world of hi-tech. Why, I ask myself, can my 10-year-old son program the VCR, but I cannot? How can my children figure out their computer games without reading the instruction booklets, and I cannot? What do I know, or remember, that hinders me from responding successfully to these new challenges?

Hardison's book clearly shows ways in which modern art celebrates technology. Modern art is typically abstract, random, kinetic (and therefore impermanent), and playful (it will not take itself too seriously). The qualities are found not only in the visual arts but in music, drama, and literature as well.

According to Hardison, "Computers complete the democratization of art begun by Dada, and as they do, they announce a change so fundamental in the idea of art that it can legitimately be called a disappearance" (219). It is the art of the television, the computer game, the synthesizer, and the computer graphics program. For instance, imagine me at my screen composing a creative work. It all moves on the scrolling computer screen. It all changes as I move around and delete words. It is easy to destroy the evidence of a bad job; I simply turn off the machine and it is gone. This technology "reminds" us of earlier ones (paper, pencil, typewriter, white-out) but it is really not like them at all. It is interactive, like a computer game; I change it all the time, so easily that I can, at times, almost be playful about it.

The technological possibilities may make us "forget" what art used to be. Take a synthesizer, for instance. What do I hear—a violin? No, I hear a synthesizer programmed to sound like a violin. Am I to remember the beautiful wood instrument, the violin? Does it matter? Will our great-grandchildren ever play violins, or will violins become rare commodities sold only at auctions and viewed mainly in museums? What will we remember? What will we forget?

Another example of new technology is hypertext, the assimilation of pieces of information on a subject into data files, like index cards for a research paper. Hypertext is a valuable memory resource; it allows us to draw from a massive library only the particular bits of information we need. It is a focused source, yet infinitely large in its possibilities. But what might hypertext cause us to forget? Hardison asks, "What does hypertext do for—or to—*The Tempest*? ... The clear implication of hypertext is that *The Tempest* is not a literary work to be enjoyed but a heap of facts to be memorized or a puzzle to be solved or a mystery to be explained. ... the play tends to disappear into the hypertext" (261–262). This is the fear of James J. Sosnoski, who worries that hypertext could turn literature into a science, "introducing by default an unwelcome 'binarism' into the study of culture" (273). Another concern is just who has the authority to create the hypertext programs and organize the files. Rather than the student, it is "the student's university professor or an anonymous programmer working for a software corporation" (Strickland 182). Meaning is not created by writers or readers but identified and embedded in the software. The possibilities of hypertext's programs dictating what students should know, value, and remember are sobering.

Hardison believes that technology may force our concept of art—our "memory" of it, and the meanings we give to the language that describes it—to radically change. Old definitions may have to be forgotten. Hardison asks these questions:

> Is the traditional concept of art still adequate for the images and music and poetry they are creating? What is the meaning in computer music of terms like "compose" and "instrument" and "perform"; in art of "artist" and "paint" and "model"; in literature of "author" and "write" and "read"? When computer art is interactive, does the consumer become the artist? When computer art is collaborative, is the machine equal in standing with the artist? Is artificial reality a work of art or is the individual who is enveloped in it the work of art? (280)

If we eliminate traditional definitions of art and are without traditional connections to it, if we must forget all we have known about understanding the arts, then where does our memory fit in? Should we just trust, then, to the much more powerful and efficient memory of the computer? No. For despite all the advantages of computer memory, shortcomings in that memory keep us from creating true artificial intelligence:

> Can a machine "understand" language? In one sense the answer is "no way." When I use the word "father" it draws a rich array of personal and cultural associations with it. I recall being held by my father when I broke my arm, going fishing with him, arguing with him, smelling his shaving lotion. I recall his death and the sense of loss that went with it. A machine never had a father. By definition it cannot "understand" in the same way that I understand. (Hardison 329)

Hardison suggests it is these memories, or as he puts it, the "series of scripts" (331) that we accumulate from childhood on that give us the consciousness that makes us human:

> No mechanism could feel pleasure at its successes, grief when its valves fuse, be warmed by flattery, be made miserable by mistakes, be charmed by sex, be angry or depressed when it cannot get what it wants. (Geoffrey Jefferson, qtd. in Hardison 344)

In *The Cultural Dimensions of Educational Computing*, C. A. Bowers refers to the "community of memory" (115). Much like Hardison's "series of scripts," his "community of memory" gives us the symbols and myths which drive our lives. To Bowers, computer technology is deficient because it "thinks" digitally rather than analogically or metaphorically, which is how human beings organize their existence (67). He fears that we will rely too much on calculation and too little on abstract, symbolic thought (205).

Another concern about the long-terms effects of computer technology is expressed by Jay David Bolter in *Writing Space: The Computer, Hypertext, and the History of Writing*. Bolter is interested is in how electronic writing changes our thinking and writing processes. These changes are dramatic, Bolter says, but raise an important question: "[A]re we left with mind-machines (computers that act like human beings) or machine-minds (human beings whose minds are computers)?" (218).

Bolter suggests that, in many ways, electronic writing comes close to the art of memory practiced by orators in Plato's time: We take our ideas and put them into spaces in memory (the computer's memory, the hypertext file). Our constantly changing society demands that we know and remember a great many facts in order to be an educated person, but now we can relegate more of these facts to external storage areas. Computer technology allows us to retrieve this information easily. It also makes the process of electronic writing much more fluid and dynamic than writing on paper. We think in new ways, Bolter suggests, ways that demand change in our mental processes and in our memories (57). In fact, he says, "the computer could dissolve Plato's distinction between internal and external memory—the distinction that is fundamental to all writing" (216).

> Electronic writing suggests a kind of writing that denies its limitations as writing and becomes unmediated thought. It would seem that writing is no longer separate from the mind, if the computer can forge an instantaneous link between the writer's thoughts and the writing surface. ... the barrier between writing and thinking dissolves and all symbolic information, anywhere in the world, is as immediately available to the writer/reader as his or her own thoughts. (217)

Bolter clearly acknowledges the possibilities afforded us by this technology. But such a change in our mental processes is not without potential danger. The dissolution of the thinking/writing barrier could lead as readily to machine-minds as to mind-machines.

Hardison's commentary on the arts and Bolter's on electronic writing treat well a situation that probably deserves more space than I've given it here. As electronic technology advances, so will our need to respond to it in philosophical as well as practical ways. Technology causes us to change the ways in which we think and the ways in which we are able to express our world. It changes how we store and retrieve *memoria*. But technology's effects are not neutral. As we create more and more sophisticated artificial intelligence, we must make sure we create machines that responsibly serve human minds and human needs. We must make sure that we retain the responsibility for what we remember.

Cultural Memory and the Media

The mainstream late-20th-century American culture fosters sameness. The media promote thin, youthful, energetic people who look, think, and talk alike. At the same time the culture promotes an orientation to the future: As in the art world, the mass culture shuns, rather than relies on, the past. We are seldom asked to memorize a memorial document like the Gettysburg Address, and we soon learn that money and success come not from remembering the past but from creating the new jingle or slogan. We discard what we no longer find useful. And if we take seriously the slogans of the media or the politicians, we may find that one of the discards is our ability to use language to express our own individuality and culture. If we give in to the seduction of the future-oriented culture, we may find that by rejecting our pasts, we have lost our memories.

At the same time, the rhetoric of mass culture beckons us with its own language to join its world. And it is hard to resist, for the conventions of language both structure memory and make thinking possible. As Michael Halloran says,

> Language is communicative because it is conventionalized, because it is an organized system of repeatable patterns which can be combined and permuted in ways that provide speaker and audience with presuppositions about what can be said without delimiting their creative potential in determining what actually is said. (630)

Language communicates to us when it evokes shared memories ("presuppositions"). In a world where many of our messages come to us via screen and amplifier, we must consider how pervasively our minds are bombarded and our thinking changed. David Marc, in "Mass Memory: The Past in the Age of Television," calls television "a throbbing public memory" that represents history, creates norms, and documents culture (127). Because television is dictated by economics, part of our mass memory is dictated by advertisers. Consumerism therefore determines our collective memory:

> By turning ... historic memorials into corporately sponsored television programs, the selling of soft drinks, automobiles, and toothpaste is put on an equal footing with the events themselves. The Constitution guarantees the spectator's freedom of speech; Coca Cola quenches the spectator's thirst. (133)

Mass culture presumes to create our memories for us: It presumes to create our *selves*.

A frightening prediction for the future comes from Neil Postman's book *Amusing Ourselves to Death: Public Discourse in the Age of Show Business*. Postman is concerned about how our minds are changed by mass media, particularly by television. The medium is the metaphor, he says, through which the content of our culture speaks. And the fact of television's existence and the way it communicates have become naturalized in our brains: We accept "knowing" through this media. Television has "achieved the status of 'myth.' ... a way of understanding the world that is not problematic, that we are not conscious of, that seems, in a word, natural" (79). Television is "so deeply embedded in our consciousness that it is invisible" (79).

Television "takes the measure of the world in twenty-two minutes" and determines the value of the news "by the number of laughs it provides" (113). It trivializes what is important, treating cultural life "as a perpetual round of entertainments" (155). Postman concludes that television has put our nation at risk. We no longer remember what real thinking is like (thinking that he says is based on our relationship to print); our memories have been changed by the medium itself.

Television creates its own myths and its own metaphors. And they are pervasive, for myth and metaphor often structure our thinking. We inhabit a "mythologically instructed community" which "provides its members with a library of scripts upon which the individual may judge the play of his multiple identities," according to Jerome Bruner (36). Culturally imposed mythological and metaphorical thinking reduces our options. Just as Neil Postman bemoans the strong effect of the entertainment culture on our thinking, Bruner believes that the requirements of technology and the rise of ideologies that subordinate the individual to the aims of the state have made it hard for a person "to create images that are satisfying in the deepest sense" (116). If there are no meaningful shared memories—if there is no stable cultural tradition—we must fabricate our own reality. Michael Halloran worries that in our disjointed modern world, without a sense of cultural wisdom, we are speechless. We have been "denied the possibility of achieving knowledge" on which to base our lives (624).

In a world where we are bombarded with information, where we must depend on external memory banks for knowledge way too profuse for us ever to absorb completely, we are silenced. When our own sense of connection or knowledge or reality seems at odds with the flow of events outside us and the prevailing "wisdom," we are silenced. We have nothing to say. We have no language with which to make ourselves understood. Our memories do not connect with our high-tech, mass-produced, and mass-promoted culture, and we cannot understand ourselves or our world.

Interestingly, one great hope for retaining diverse loyalties and interests may come from the media itself, because of the diversification made possible by new technologies. When we can receive 30 or 100 channels on our televisions instead of 6 or 7, we are assured of some difference. In fact, competitive television has expanded the number of "communities" we are able to flip to: fishermen and hunters, science aficionados, home crafters, foreign language speakers, and regional enthusiasts. Consumed wisely, the television provides us not just with the monolithic cultural mainstays but with many diverse and important options.

Speaking about the more monolithic side of the media, however, poet and screenwriter Michael Ventura suggests that it is hostile to memory. It "thrives on nostalgia," a "vague, sentimental wash that obscures memory and acts as a narcotic to dull the importance of the present" (176). The media rewrites history, and, because technology makes it so easy replace or recreate, it is easy for it to lie. "Media is the history that forgives," Ventura says. "It is the impulse to redeem the past … by presenting it as we would have most liked it to be" (181). James Baldwin's 1963 "A Talk to Teachers" makes clear, for instance, that the myths the White society have created about Blacks act to oppress them: the Black child grows up in the land of freedom and opportunity, but is at the same time "assured by his country and his countrymen that he has never contributed anything to civilization— that his past is nothing more than a record of humiliations gladly endured" (4). The White American creates an identity out of "a series of myths about one's heroic ancestors" (9), glorifying ancestors rather than admitting (or remembering) the truth about some of this country's European born settlers: "They were hungry, they were poor, they were convicts" (9). Americans who live this myth, Baldwin says, have lost their grip on reality. What is lost is a connection with a real past and a real present and therefore a sense of identity. This is where modern mainstream American culture seems to depart most completely from the cultures of its ancestors, and this is what modern America must reclaim if it is to have a future:

> Unless a body of thought connects with a living ground, there is no possibility that this era will discover itself within its cacophony and create, one day, a post-AD culture. … We are not only dying. We are living. And we are struggling to share our lives, which is all, finally, that "culture" means. (Ventura 188)

Culture means sharing our lives, which means sharing our memories.

Many marginalized societies value memory to a greater extent than the mainstream American culture does. Paula Gunn Allen shows the contrast between cultures as she writes about contemporary Native American communities:

> [Contemporary Indian communities] believe that the roots of oppression are to be found in the loss of tradition and memory because that loss is always accompanied by a loss of a positive sense of self. In short, Indians think it is important to remember, while Americans believe it is important to forget. (15)

Paradoxically, it is by adopting the attitudes toward memory of the marginalized cultures that we can begin to see the value of our individual cultural memory in creating identity, in unsilencing voices, and in defending ourselves against mass culture's thinking.

As mass media and international communications bring our world closer together, uniformity threatens to become oppressive. We lose the freshness offered by diversity, and, at the same time, we lose the real sense of sharing offered by common tradition. And we lose the creative tension between the two when uniformity comes from an outside world which only vaguely relates to our experience. We are the losers when we give up the important resources that memory provides. For example, we must remember that our society has protected freedom of speech and provided for the latitude to contemplate varied and unconventional attitudes and discourses in a free atmosphere. We cannot afford to lose this freedom. We cannot by lolled into forgetfulness or narrow-mindedness by a seductive mass culture. To battle nostalgia, false myths, and uniformity, we must look critically at language. Only when we understand how powerfully the images created by our language control the structure of memory can we and our students begin to resist those structures and work from a deeper, more meaningful memory as we attempt to interpret our world.

Remembering in Other Mainstreams

The mass culture, in its infatuation with the present moment and the future, appears to have lost interest in hanging on to traditions and to knowledge about our pasts. Yet the rhetorics of many other cultures show clearly that understanding the discourse depends on sharing in the cultural memory from which the rhetoric arises. Following are examples of different ways in which this works. Considering these examples may remind those of us tempted by mass culture's appeal to remember our own roots; forgetting our pasts is not a prerequisite for facing our future.

The link between memory and language is vividly seen in the experiences of the bilingual person. Min-zhan Lu, in her essay "From Silence to Words: Writing as Struggle," shows the influence of culture, family, and words themselves on her thinking as she grows up bilingual in China. Her upbringing imprinted on her memory forms for writing as well as meanings for words such as "class," "consciousness," and "bourgeois." The politicizing of her native language forced it to lose its spontaneity for her: It silenced her. She worries now for her daughter in an American composition classroom where she has succeeded at writing "as a survival tool." Lu regrets this metaphor and believes students are taught to "ignore those voices that seem irrelevant to the purified world of the classroom." She advocates instead that we

> encourage students to explore ways of practicing the conventions of the discourse they are learning by negotiating through those conflicting voices. We could also encourage them to see themselves as responsible for forming or transforming as well as preserving the discourse they are learning. (447)

She is encouraging the composition classroom to respect the different discourses that come from different experiences, different memories.

Min-zhan Lu's frustrations could be those of any bilingual or bicultural student, even if the two languages were standard English and an American dialect. But inherent in the Chinese language is another factor that links those who grow up with it to the particular culture in stronger ways than do many other languages: the memorization necessary to be literate in Chinese. Carolyn Matalene explains this phenomenon in "Contrastive Rhetoric: An American Writing Teacher in China." The Chinese language consists of some 43,000 characters (791), some of which stand for words, some for syllables. Just to read a newspaper entails knowing 3,000 to 5,000 characters (792). More than the 26 letters of our alphabet must be stored in memory. In addition, Chinese education has traditionally been based on memorization rather than on interpretation: "The usual Chinese response to a literary text is to repeat it, not to paraphrase, analyze, or interpret it" (791). Learning means "learning the text by heart" (791). Literacy also implies knowledge of a host of proverbs and maxims that traditionally sprinkle conversation and writing. "Thus," Matalene tells us,

> for the Chinese writer, style means manipulating one's memory bank of phrases, arrangement means fitting the forms, and invention means doing it the way it has been done. Each the these three arts of rhetoric depends profoundly on the fourth, memory. (794)

Chinese students not only memorize the language; "they memorize the culture itself" (792).

Matalene suggests that receptiveness to a multiplicity of voices must include understanding of the voice that brings with it a heritage in which memory and memorization are central to rhetoric and culture.

Memory plays a vital role in African and African-American rhetorics, too, for both are linked closely to orality, according to Molefi Kete Asante in *The Afrocentric Idea*. Form and substance are not separate, and the speech act depends much on delivery for its meaning. In that sense, it is poetic in nature. And both African and African-American rhetorics depend on myths—on shared memory—to make meaning. Asante maintains that "mythos," the Greek word from which "myth" comes, originally meant "utterance." It is precisely because these 'deep utterances' operate at unconscious levels that they maintain our symbolic life at a conscious level" (96).

Myths, kept up through stories, tales, and rituals, supply "the abundance of cultural memory" in both African and African-American societies (Asante 99). This shared memory is the basis for Black resistance rhetoric today, Asante says. Instead of trying to speak like their oppressors, resisters choose to use their own language, which is based as much on myth as the language of their African ancestors. Through the stories of these heroes who can transcend the American experience, they keep the history of oppression in the foreground (Asante 81); they remember it. Their "guerilla rhetoric tactics" demand that to understand the language, a person has to share the memory, has to know the words, myths, legends and sounds of the African-American experience (116).

One rhetorical strategy that is utterly dependent on shared memory is *signifying,* or "the act of linguistic misdirection" (Bizzell and Herzberg 1192), which turns words away from their literal (White) meaning to a metaphoric (Black) meaning.

It is an art of indirection and wit. Henry Louis Gates, Jr., explains Signifyin(g)—his capital S and parentheses serve to distinguish this term from the "White" word—in *The Signifying Monkey: A Theory of Afro-American Criticism.* The Monkey, he tells us, "is a hero of black myth, a sign of triumph of wit and reason, his language of Signifyin(g) standing as the linguistic sign of the ultimate triumph of self-consciously formal language use (1214). The Monkey, then, is the ultimate guerilla, using language as his weapon. Signifyin(g) says one thing and means another. Only those who share an understanding of Signifyin(g) can decode it, and the decoding works on two levels: First, a person has to know that Signifyin(g) is taking place; second, that person has to share the interpretation of the speaker. So Signifyin(g) is not only meaning, but a way of meaning as well. Signifyin(g) is the master trope; Gates says it subsumes all other black rhetorical tropes, which include "marking, loud-talking, testifying, calling out (of one's name), sounding, rapping, playing the dozens" (1199). Signifyin(g) revises meaning based on shared memory and understanding. It serves to maintain the connectedness of the culture through language while excluding the outsider/oppressor and to liberate its users from their positions of silence in the outsiders' world.

Paulo Freire's liberation pedagogy is another attempt to revise rhetoric, and it underscores the importance of memory to that end. Critical consciousness allows one to name the world, an act which encompasses not only action but reflection as well. Perceiving facts, Freire says, always means recognizing their relation to other facts; this recognition is the act of interpretation, an act of memory. "'Human beings are not just what they are, but also what they were': they are in a state of being" (Freire 132). Ann Berthoff explicates Freire's critical consciousness, or "conscientization":

> Paulo Freire's pedagogy of the oppressed offers a revolutionary model for the Third World because it provides a method which does not depend on knowledge that has been "deposited" (in Freire's best-known metaphor of education as banking); rather it is a method by which learners call upon their capacities as creatures who live in history: they reclaim their powers as language animals, the species-specific power to name the world—to read the world, to write the world. These are all acts of mind: naming, reading, writing are, of course, actual linguistic operations, but they are simultaneously metaphors for interpretation. ("Paulo Freire's" 364)

The greatest mission of a liberation pedagogy is clearing the memory back of the deposits of an oppressive culture, reactivating the individual memory, and thus reactivating a true cultural memory.

Memory is the key to identity. The importance of remembering is clearly illustrated in Toni Morrison's novel *Beloved.* Morrison uses the term *disremember* to express the purposeful repression of the past. The past is too painful, too complicated, to deal with, so it is disremembered. Yet Morrison confronts her protagonist Sethe with the living ghost of her murdered daughter, forcing Sethe to face her own history. Only in "rememory"—in bringing back and dealing with the repressed—can a person *live*, Morrison tells us. The past is a necessary part of a person's present identity and must be acknowledged.

Native American writer M. Scott Momaday, in his book *The Way to Rainy Mountain*, tells of the Kiowas' journey from Yellowstone to Rainy Mountain. On the way, the tribe was able to develop an idea of who they were as a people: "they were able through words to imagine an identity in their existential act of self-creation" (Velie 28). Momaday's book testifies to the importance of words and the oral tradition and therefore the *remembering* that is crucial to the oral tradition: "as long as the story of the journey is told, they exist as a distinct people and culture" (Velie 28). Momaday says in the book, "The journey herein recalled continues to be made anew each time the miracle comes to mind, for that is peculiarly the right and responsibility of the imagination" (4, qtd. in Velie 28).

Along with the importance of telling stories, Momaday also acknowledges the importance of *naming* in Native American culture. Names, of course, are based on the perspective of those who do the naming; naming reflects a whole world view, a cultural memory. Benjamin Whorf says that naming is:

> no act of unfettered imagination, even in the wildest flights of nonsense, but a strict use of already patterned materials. If asked to invent forms not already prefigured in the patternment of his [sic] language, the speaker is negative in the same manner as if asked to make fried eggs without eggs. (qtd. in Spender 163)

Momaday's mother had no Indian blood after her great-grandmother, yet she considered herself Indian and called herself "Little Moon." Momaday himself was given the name "Rock Tree Boy." The names, he believes, allowed them to think of themselves as Indian, to remember their Indian heritage: "This act of imagination was, I believe, among the most important events of my mother's early life, as later the same essential act was to be the most important of my own" (qtd. in Velie 17). This act is the "power to name the world" that Paulo Freire mentioned; it is acknowledged by mainstream western writers such as Heidegger, Nietzsche, Proust, and Derrida. "[T]he past never seems to be fully lost in the signifying process of a proper name—the present moment of signification is resonant with past usages and past associations" (Hurlbert 19).

Many Native American writers, like Leslie Marmon Silko in *Ceremony* and Louise Erdrich in *Love Medicine*, bring back the names and the stories of the forgotten past specifically to help recreate an identity for lost people. They show the exile of reservation Native Americans, caught between the worlds of past and present, but unable to identify with either. Yet identification with the past is necessary for a sense of personal identity.

The names, the words, and the stories which resonate with memories give each of us that sense of identity. Again, as Kenneth Burke says in *A Rhetoric of Motives*, the purpose of rhetoric today is not persuasion but identification. "Identification is compensatory to division. If men were not apart from one another, there would be no need for the rhetorician to proclaim their unity" (1020). In a world of alienation, a sense of identity is what most of us desire.

Lest a reader think that this desire to recreate the past is simply nostalgic, a statement from Gayle Greene's "Feminist Fiction and the Uses of Memory" is useful and fitting for discussing any subordinated history:

In fact, nostalgia and remembering are in some sense antithetical, since nostalgia is a forgetting, merely regressive, whereas memory may look back in order to move forward and transform disabling fictions to enabling fictions, altering our relation to the present and future. (298)

Memory leads to identification with our past and our culture which leads not to sentimentality but to empowerment.

Learning From Feminist Rhetoric

Empowerment has been the ultimate goal of the women's movement. In the past, women's lack of empowerment has been inextricably bound up in language. Women have been muted by a language created by and privileging men. The result has been, for the most part, silence. In *Women's Ways of Knowing*, Belenky, Clinchy, Goldberger and Tarule explain how silenced women have no sense of we-ness, of connectedness with others, of shared experience (27). We could say that they have no sense of a shared cultural memory: They have been kept isolated, and they don't know what they know. Therefore, they accept roles of extreme powerlessness. In *The Feminine Mystique*, Betty Friedan refers to the malaise of the 1950s housewife as "the problem that has no name" (qtd. in Greene 299); the malaise is "a loss of memory, of the ability to experience 'the dimensions of both past and future'" (Greene 300). The research done for *Women's Ways of Knowing* shows that silence is the "unifying theme" (19) of the women whom the authors studied, and, at the same time, that "women repeatedly used the metaphor of voice to depict their intellectual and ethical development; and that the development of a sense of voice, mind, and self were intricately intertwined" (18).

No voice, no mind, no self. And what Betty Friedan calls a loss of memory is equally a loss of history, or what Gayle Greene calls a "collective amnesia" (298), for the history of women's struggle for rights and equality has been regularly muffled. Adrienne Rich calls it "the erasure of women's political and historical past"; Nancy Cott calls it "a disremembering process" (qtd. in Greene 298). Consciousness-raising, Greene says, is a "re-membering, a bringing to mind of repressed parts of the self and experience" (300). The process is often expressed in archeological terms: excavating, digging, or, like the speaker in Adrienne Rich's poem, diving into the wreck. Such excavating, Greene tells us, gives us a new kind of memory that allows us "to construct alternatives for the future" (300–301). It is a means to empowerment.

Although writing is an empowering activity, even women who write have been silenced in many ways. Dale Spender observes that women's writing has traditionally been in the private sphere—which includes writing for other women:

That women should restrict their writing to the private realm may have been an understanding that was constructed by males and one which may have been policed by males, but it is nonetheless one which women have been obliged to share, to come to terms with, and even perhaps to internalize. (195)

Women have shared in this myth; they've taken on male definitions of the world and they judge by male standards. By internalizing these male perceptions—by accepting them as valid *memoria*—they have allowed themselves to believe that men are better than women, Spender says (197).

Acceptance of externally imposed standards also means living with taboos. Many women writers note the reality of these taboos as they write. Adrienne Rich, in the foreword to a collection of essays written by women artists and scientists about their work, quotes the following from an MLA panel speech given by Susan Griffin:

> I think that writers are always dealing with taboos of one sort or another; if they are not taboos general in society, you may just have a fear in your private life of perceiving some truth because of its implications, and that will stop you from writing. ... And for a writer, the most savage censor is oneself. (xx)

Griffin's lesbianism is what made her particularly feel the taboos around her, but the awareness of taboos and the fear of breaking them is true of many women. In the same volume, writer Tillie Olsen says that women have extreme pressures to censor their own voices and go with dominant attitudes (329).

Unfortunately, censoring their own voices and going with the dominant attitude has often been the prescription given in writing classes for any female or male students who don't comfortably call the dominant discourse their own. It is a choice suggested from the outside by those who accept only the structures and conventions of certain academic discourses; it is a conscious choice of many muted students who feel that their powerlessness comes from the subordinate status of their language. It is the solution that Margaret Pigott came to in a 1979 article in which she concludes that male students like wide-context subjects and do lots of generalizing, whereas female students tend to write about themselves. She suggests that females have "unique problems in thinking" (927) and that writing teachers should have female students practice tagmemic invention, inductive reasoning, and thesis statement writing to get rid of their "limitations." She may be right—if mastering the prevailing academic discourse is the main goal.

If going with the dominant discourse occurs at the expense of one's own voice, it is an inferior choice and a detrimental one. It is detrimental because it demands the "disremembering" of one's own experiences and because it asks students to adopt a language without meaning to them yet. Joan Bolker gives a name to the academic writing she often gets from girls who adopt this language: the Griselda Syndrome. The papers show lack of personality and sense of ownership, "a style that aims to please and offends none ... shows very little of a thought process, but strives instead to produce a neat package tied with a ribbon" (907). Griselda's paper is "a compulsive gesture toward closure and ritual, an exchange of 'self' for 'success' in the academic economy" (Juncker 429). Richard Haswell, in "Dark Shadows: The Fate of the Writer at the Bottom," talks not just about women but about any student who has trouble writing in the discourse. He says writers learn to turn in "stout writing," which is thoughtless and vapid but acceptable and hard to criticize because it follows the conventions. He says that we should worry more about truth and accuracy in writing and less about forms. These concerns are not new; they echo Emig's earlier complaint about the memoryless composing of school-sponsored writing.

Truth and accuracy are possible only when memory is invoked. We can write about only what we experience. We can draw truly and accurately only from that which is a part of our personal and cultural understanding of the world. And we can write about it only in a language that has the words to express it. Again, we are brought back to the idea of naming. Dale Spender says that "names which cannot draw on past meanings are meaningless" (161). If the world has been named by a culture that does not share our view of the world, its language cannot express our views. We must rename.

Renaming has been the goal of the efforts to establish feminist rhetoric. Carol Gilligan calls it "a different voice," and argues that woman's voice needs to be heard and recognized for "the different perspective it brings to bear on the construction and resolution of moral problems" (482); concepts of responsibility and care are central to the woman's moral domain, and they need to be heard. Deborah Tannen believes that just knowing the differences typical of men and women in conversation can breed respect and can allow men and women to get beyond language differences "to confront real conflicts of interest—and to find a shared language in which to negotiate them" (18). Mary Daly's *Gyn/Ecology* wants us to "look behind the taken-for-granted words, so she restructures them: re-member, crone-logical, the/rapist, a-maze" (Cameron 6). Dale Spender says that women must name and write about the parts of their lives—the drudgery and caretaking, for instance—that have been "non-existent in the minds of men" (222). Renaming in all these cases involves looking critically at what language already says—and what it leaves unexpressed. It is not an easy task. As Adrienne Rich says, "The awakening of consciousness is not like the crossing of a frontier—one step and you are in another country" ("When" 2055). Our memories are too loaded down with the paraphernalia—the names, myths, and metaphors—of the land our consciousnesses called home. But the renaming is the key to breaking the silence, to revising the discourse.

Helene Cixous sees in writing "*the very possibility of change, the space that can serve as a springboard for subversive thought …*" (249). Clara Juncker suggests that we must have our students do activities that make them aware of the openness of, the possibilities in, writing. We must encourage students "to play with language, to stretch it, form it, caress it" in order to return to them "the pleasure of the text" (Juncker 432). She quotes Cixous' *The Newly Born Woman*:

> There will not be *one* feminine discourse, there will be thousands of different kinds of feminine words, and then there will be the code for general communication, philosophical discourse, rhetoric like now but with a great number of subversive discourses in addition that are somewhere else entirely. (137, qtd. in Juncker 434)

That "somewhere else entirely" may be the memory stores of a world of not just women but all potential writers with stories to tell in their own words. "Remembering and telling are generative and restorative acts that endow the past with flesh, blood, and a heartbeat. By 'going inside,' then reaching outside and telling by memory and narration" (Greene 318), we can expand our understanding of the world and culturally empower those whose thought and experience have been marginalized or muted by the constraints of any dominant language and its conventions.

Reclaiming Memory in the Rhetoric of the University

The university, presumedly the home of diverse thinking and free speech, has traditionally fostered dominant discourses. Therefore, women have found it hard to get ahead unless they adapt the "universal" and "logical" discourses of the men who surround them. Bizzell and Herzberg speak to this problem as it relates to women's scholarly work in rhetoric and composition; it applies to the classroom as well:

> To the extent that women use the prevailing philosophical or disciplinary discourses, that is, to the extent that women's work looks like men's work, the hitherto reflexive prejudice against women intellectuals has effectively disappeared (though pockets of resistance doubtless remain). The second issue, though, raises the question of whether women abandon a distinctive women's rhetoric to engage in men's (that is, traditional academic) rhetoric. This question applies as well to areas of social life other than the academy, particularly to business and government, where the traditional discourse has been shaped by men. (919)

In her book *Textual Carnivals: The Politics of Composition*, Susan Miller addresses the question of powerlessness or exclusion as it relates to the whole field of composition and the teaching of writing (a field which, interestingly, has been dominated by women). She contends that the separation of composition and literature has been devastating for composition. The split has emphasized the difference between literature, or good writing (that which is to be read and remembered) and composition, or bad writing (that which students write and which we all should forget). Everyone involved in composition—in reading and teaching writing that remains forgettable—is marginalized, Miller says (85). Students are usually taught "standard" writing practices, without being taught "the agendas of these communities for including and excluding particular alternative interpretations or standards" (9). Students have no sense of creating "significant pieces of writing"; in fact, the composition course "was set up to be a national course in silence" (55). Often the department itself remains in silence, too.

In a chapter called "The Sad Woman in the Basement," Miller details the problems that composition teachers (two thirds of whom are women) have in achieving any of the signs of status: tenure, money, respect. Like most possessions sent to the basement, the teachers of composition, along with the essays of their students, are forgotten.

Yet surfacing from the cellar and breaking the silence are the only ways to be remembered. Miller explains as she introduces her book:

> I have come to understand the politics of writing by learning that power is, at its roots, telling our own stories. Without "good" stories to rely on, no minority or marginalized majority has a chance to change its status, or, more importantly, to identify and question the "bad" tales that create it. (1)

This is the message implicit in James Berlin's essay "Composition Studies and Cultural Studies: Collapsing Boundaries." Berlin contends that cultural studies have taken over the role traditionally played by rhetoric: to show how language is used in the service of power. He says that cultural studies is about "the historical forms of consciousness or subjectivity" (4), which is to say that cultural studies is about the cultural memory and the way the individual memory is framed by it. Composition studies can do this, too. "The semiotic codes needed for text production and consumption are obviously complex and varied," Berlin tells us, "and it will be the business of rhetoric to develop lexicons to articulate them in order to teach effective strategies for writing and reading" (21). Effective strategies are those that teach resistance, those that teach students to recognize the limitations on their thinking and interpretation prescribed by language, conventions, and culture. The writing class is the place to "intervene" in the process of text production and make students aware of whose language they are using (28). Berlin quotes Mark Hurlbert and Michael Blitz' *Composition and Resistance* to show how writing can be "a political act of transformation and betterment":

> If we can do anything as writing teachers and as writers, it should be to stop teaching students to underwrite the university, to stop demanding written material which can be easily gathered and assessed. We can teach writing as an event in which knowledge and form is preserved or resisted and changed. We can teach writing as the material out of which we not only (re)create ourselves and others, our understanding of culture, ethnicity, gender, sexuality, class, but also as the material with which we can resist these narratives when they do not accurately reflect our real lives. (Berlin 30; Hurlbert and Blitz 7)

Hurlbert and Blitz later suggest that "as counter-educators we can teach students to challenge the ways that formal education *fixes* what people say and do and think" (170). What we see here is a real effort to recognize the influences on memory—on the ideas, conventions, and notions from which we write—in order to clarify what comes from the dominant culture, what from our own culture, and what from our individual life amidst the two. Then we can have writing which teaches us to see beyond boundaries. We will be able to see in new ways. But the rhetorics that are new will not be rejections of the past. Instead, they will be blends of the diverse pasts, presents and futures of their creators.

Robert de Beaugrande, in "In Search of Feminist Discourse: The 'Difficult' Case of Luce Irigaray" says that "Language subjects the world to a barely resistible power to posit, designate, signify, and organize" (257). This power can be used to empower, or to marginalize or exclude:

> Here lies the real crux of the matter, and it concerns everyone. ... Does the relation between language and the "world" retain enough leeway to allow a substantive remodeling of our consciousness? Can we get free enough from language to watch it at work and introduce a new balance? Can we deregulate the functioning of discourse so that its limits could be differently drawn? Can we deconstruct our entrenched conceptions, and the discourses that presuppose them, to the point where a genuinely non-aligned system of discourse might enable a free and commensurate communication among all humans ... ? (257)

We must optimistically answer these questions "yes." Only if we treat these ideas as serious goals can we write, and foster in others, *memorial* writing: writing that rings true, writing in which language reflects meaning which reflects real experience.

Conclusion

Let me tell you a story. I am in a classroom. It's hot and muggy, and I'm tired. I am not the teacher but the student. We are discussing possible paper topics on subjects related to rhetoric. The instructor suggests memory and delivery, enthusiastically pointing out their potential. I perk up for a moment; I've been worried about my memory, and the notion of trying to fill up my own mental rooms and memorizing the contents has a certain crazy appeal. But we move on, and I don't even write down the idea.

I remember that moment later, however, and it leads to the discussion that begins this book—a friend and I are musing about memory. The end of the story is the book you have before you.

In it, you've been given a long survey of memory from many perspectives. Why have I compiled it? I've done so because I'm convinced that memory is truly our Muse. It's a creative force, it's respected across disciplines, and it deserves our reconsideration. We'll do a better job of teaching our students to write if we understand how much memory is involved in the whole writing process.

Going back to the history of rhetoric shows that *memory*, like *rhetoric*, has more than one meaning. The meanings range from the *Ad Herennium*'s concept of memorizing specific words and images to Plato's idea that memory holds our intellectual ability to make meaning out of language and experience. To see memory as a generative force in the production of writing is not a new idea at all, but one of many time-honored ways of looking at it. Even today, and maybe especially today, memory is a valid part of a complete rhetoric. It is crucial to invention and important to arrangement, style, and delivery as well.

From Freudian psychoanalysis to the latest scientific research, studies confirm that memory helps to create and continually re-create our knowledge base. The more scientists study both language and the human brain, the clearer the connection becomes between language, thought, expression, and memory.

Through their explanations of social or collective memory, both philosophers and psychologists broaden our understanding of the rhetoric of our culture and the preconceptions with which students sometimes approach writing. Understanding this larger memory gives us new ways to help students identify and use—or break out of—patterns and assumptions embedded in memory.

Memory is a critical part of interpretation, knowledge, and language itself. Teaching students to use their memories when they write is a way to reconnect writing with *thought* and to reduce the perception of writing instruction as the teaching of arrangement and style. It's a way to help students see how their own thoughts connect with the issues of the world around them.

As philosophers probe for answers to the dilemma of modern alienation, postmodern writers show us the alienation in their works. They all look to language as a source of this anguish and, at the same time, the hope for overcoming it. Language allows us to remember and therefore to understand. Heidegger tells us that memory is the gathering of thought and that thought is made possible by language. Only when we understand how thoroughly language shapes thinking can we begin to free our thoughts, and then our language, of constraints.

Memory can be the muse for all writers. It is only a small step from poetry to argument, and a muse crucial to poets can be equally valuable for persuasive writers. Remembering leads to inspiration and to understanding. Life makes sense not when we live it but when we remember it. It is a logical next step to suggest that we encourage both remembering and understanding through writing. We bring our memory to reading, too. Interpretation—our way of reading both texts and reading life—is accomplished through memory.

As we all try to lead meaningful lives in the 21st century culture, we need to understand and then resist forces, including patterns of language use, that alienate us from our own experience. We will succeed in the culture only if we share in its making. We can begin to do so by demanding that its language reflect the real worlds—the memories made and to be made—of the citizens who inhabit it. As writing teachers we have a tremendous opportunity to influence attitudes towards language and writing and therefore to help students become active in shaping our language-dependent world.

Culture and history (in a word, *memory*) cannot be removed from language. Language always reflects someone's culture, someone's history. Language fails when it denies its users connections with their own cultures and histories. To overcome this failure, we must revise our use of that language, our rhetoric. And revision will occur quite naturally if we attend carefully to memory as we prepare to write. We must stalwartly resist meaningless language and meaningless forms. We must re-member, re-collect, re-construct, and re-interpret our world as it is created through language and experience. In doing so, we may find that all those words that give us power to speak and to be understood—*language, interpretation, knowledge*—are no more, and no less, than synonyms for memory.

References

Abbott, Don Paul. "Rhetoric and Writing in Renaissance Europe and England." In *A Short History of Writing Instruction From Ancient Greece to Twentieth Century America*. Ed. James J. Murphy. Davis, CA: Hermagoras Press, 1990. 95–120.

Ackerman, Diane. "Oh Muse! You Do Make Things Difficult!" *New York Times Review of Books* 12 Nov. 1989: 1+.

Albertus Magnus. *De Bono*. In *Opera Omnia* (XXVII). Ed. H. Kuhle, C. Feckes, B. Geyer, adn W. Kubel. Monasterii Westfalorum: in Aedibus Aschendorff, 1951. 82 ff.

Allen, Paula Gunn. "Who is Your Mother? Red Roots of White Feminism." In Simonson and Walker 13–27.

Anderson, John R. *Cognitive Psychology and Its Implications*. 2nd ed. New York: W. H. Freeman, 1985.

Angeles, Peter A. *Dictionary of Philosophy*. New York: Barnes and Noble, 1981.

Aquinas, Saint Thomas. *The Summa Theologica of St. Thomas Aquinas*. 2nd ed. London: Burns, Oates and Washbourne, 1935.

Aristotle. *On Memory*. In *The Complete Works of Aristotle* Vol. 1. ed. Jonathan Barnes. Princeton: Princeton University Press, 1984: 714–720.

———. *Poetics*. Trans. Gerald Else. Ann Arbor: University of Michigan Press, 1967.

———. *The Rhetoric of Aristotle*. Trans. Lane Cooper. Englewood Cliffs, NJ: Prentice-Hall, 1932.

Aronson, Eliot. *The Social Animal*. 5th ed. New York: W.H. Freeman, 1988.

Asante, Molefi K. *The Afrocentric Idea*. Philadelphia: Temple University Press, 1987.

Augustine, Saint. *The Confessions of Saint Augustine*. In *The Essential Augustine*. Ed. V.J. Bourke. New York: Mentor–Omega Books, 1964.

———. *On Christian Doctrine*. Trans. D. W. Robinson, Jr. Indianapolis: Bobbs Merrill Educ. Publishing, 1958.

———. *On the Trinity*. In *The Essential Augustine*. Ed. V.J. Bourke. New York: Mentor–Omega Books, 1964.

Axelrod, Rise B., and Charles Cooper. *The St. Martin's Guide to Writing*. 2nd ed. New York: St. Martin's Press, 1988.

Ayer, A. J. *Philosophy in the Twentieth Century*. New York: Random House, 1982.

Bacon, Francis. *The Advancement of Learning*. In *The Philosophical Works of Francis Bacon*. Ed. J. M. Robertson. New York: E.P. Dutton, 1905.

Baldwin, James. "A Talk to Teachers." In Simonson and Walker 3–12.

Bannister, Donald, and John M. M. Mair. *The Evaluation of Personal Constructs*. New York: Academic Press, 1968.

Barclay, Craig. "Schematization of Autobiographical Memory." In Rubin 82–97.

Barrett, William, and Henry D. Aiken. *Philosophy in the Twentieth Century*. 4 vols. New York: Random House, 1962.

Bartlett, Frederick C. *Remembering: A Study in Experimental and Social Psychology*. Cambridge: Cambridge University Press, 1932.

Beaugrande, Robert de. "In Search of Feminist Discourse: The 'Difficult' Case of Lucy Irigaray." *College English* 50 (1988): 253–272.

Belenky, Mary Field, Blythe McVicker Clinchy, Nancy Rule Goldberger, and Jill Mattuck Tarule. *Women's Ways of Knowing*. New York: Basic Books, 1986.

Benjamin, Ludy T., Jr., J. Roy Hopkins, and Jack R. Nation. *Psychology*. 2nd ed. New York: MacMillan, 1990.

Bennett, Edward Armstrong. *C. G. Jung*. New York: E.P. Dutton, 1962.

Benson, Thomas W., and Michael H. Prosser. *Readings in Classical Rhetoric*. Davis, CA: Hermagoras Press, 1988.

Bereiter, Carl, and Marlene Scardamalia. *The Psychology of Written Composition*. Hillsdale, NJ: Lawrence Erlbaum Associates, 1987.

Berkeley, George. *A Treatise Concerning the Principles of Human Knowledge*. Ed. Colin M. Turbayne. New York: Liberal Arts Press, 1957.

Berlin, James A. "Composition Studies and Cultural Studies: Collapsing Boundaries." In *Into the Field: Sites of Composition Studies*. Ed. Anne Ruggles Gere. New York: Modern Language Association, 1993.

————. "Rhetoric and Ideology in the Writing Classroom." *College English* 50.5 (1988): 477–493.

Berthoff, Ann E. *The Making of Meaning*. Upper Montclair, NJ: Boynton/Cook, 1981.

————. "Paulo Freire's Liberation Pedagogy." *Language Arts* 67.4 (1990): 362–369.

————, ed. *Reclaiming the Imagination: Philosophical Perspectives for Writers and Teachers of Writing*. Portsmouth, NH: Boynton/Cook, 1984.

————. "Rhetoric as Hermeneutic." *College Composition and Communication* 42.3 (1991): 279–287.

Birault, Henri. "Thinking and Poetizing in Heidegger." In *On Heidegger and Language*. Ed. Joseph J. Kockelmans. Evanston, IL: Northwestern University Press, 1972, 147–168.

Bizzell, Patricia and Bruce Herzberg. *The Rhetorical Tradition: Readings in Classical Rhetoric from Classical Times to the Present*. Boston: Bedford Books, 1990.

Bleich, David. *Readings and Feelings: An Introduction to Subjective Criticism*. Urbana, IL: National Council of Teachers of English, 1975.

————. *Subjective Criticism*. Baltimore: Johns Hopkins University Press, 1978.

Block, Haskell M., and Herman Salinger. *The Creative Vision: Modern European Writers on Their Art*. New York: Grove Press, 1960.

Bolker, Joan. "Teaching Griselda to Write." *College English* 40 (1979): 906–908.

Bolter, Jay David. "Hypertext and the Rhetorical Canons." In Reynolds, *Rhetorical Memory and Delivery* 97–112.

————. *Writing Space: The Computer, Hypertext, and the History of Writing*. Hillsdale: Lawrence Erlbaum Associates, 1991.

Booth, Wayne C. *Critical Understanding: The Limits and Powers of Pluralism*. Chicago: University of Chicago Press, 1979.

————. *The Rhetoric of Fiction*. Chicago: University of Chicago Press, 1961.

Bowers, C. A. *The Cultural Dimensions of Educational Computing: The Non-Neutrality of Teachnology*. New York: Teachers College Press, 1988.

Bowie, Malcolm. *Freud, Proust and Lacan: Theory as Fiction*. New York: Cambridge University Press, 1987.

Brand, Alice G. "The Why of Cognition: Emotion and the Writing Process." *College Composition and Composition* 38 (1987): 436–443.

Britton, James. "Shaping at the Point of Utterance." In *Reinventing the Rhetorical Tradition*. Ed. Aviva Freedman and Ian Pringle. Conway, AR: L & S Books, 1980. Rpt. in *Learning to Write*. Ed. Aviva Freedman, Ian Pringle, and J. Yalden. New York: Longman, 1983, 13–19.

Bruffee, Kenneth. "Collaborative Learning and the Conversation of Mankind." *College English*, 45 (1984):635–652.

Bruner, Jerome S. *On Knowing: Essays for the Left Hand*. Cambridge: Belknap Press, 1979.

Burke, Kenneth. *A Rhetoric of Motives*. Berkeley: University of California Press, 1969. Excerpted in Bizzell and Herzberg 1018–1034.

Calendrillo, Linda T. *The Art of Memory and Rhetoric*. Diss. Purdue University, 1988. Ann Arbor, MI: University Microfilms International, 1991. 8900638.

Cameron, Deborah. *Feminism and Linguistic Theory*. New York: St. Martin's Press, 1985.

Campbell, Jeremy. *Grammatical Man: Information, Entropy, Language and Life*. New York: Simon and Schuster, 1982.

Campbell, Joseph. *The Masks of God: Creative Mythology*. New York: Penguin Books, 1968.

Carruthers, Mary J. *The Book of Memory: A Study of Memory in Medieval Culture*. New York: Cambridge University Press, 1990.

Castell, Alburey, and Donald M. Borchert. *An Introduction to Modern Philosophy: Examining the Human Condition*. 5th ed. New York: MacMillan, 1988.

Chomsky, Noam. *Language and Mind*. New York: Harcourt Brace Jovanovich, 1972.

Christie, Norton Bradley. *Another War and Postmodern Memory: Remembering Vietnam*. Diss. Duke University 1988. Ann Arbor, MI: University Microfilms International, 1991. 8822010.

Cicero. *De Oratore*. 2 vols. Trans. E. W. Sutton & H. Rackham. Cambridge: Harvard University Press, 1942.

Cixous, Helene. "The Laugh of the Medusa." *Signs* 1 (1976): 875–893.

Coleridge, Samuel Taylor. *Biographia Literaria*. New York: E.P. Dutton, 1938.

Collins, Alan F., Susan Gathercole, Martin A. Conway, and Peter E. Morris, eds. *Theories of Memory*. Hillsdale, NJ: Lawrence Erlbaum Associates, 1995.

Connors, Robert J. "Personal Writing Assignments." *College Composition and Communication* 38.2: 166–183.

Conway, Martin A., and David C. Rubin. "The Structure of Autobiography." In Collins, Gathercole, Conway and Morris 103–137.

Coover, Robert. "The Babysitter." In *The Norton Anthology of Short Fiction*. 4th ed. Ed. R. V. Cassill. New York: W. W. Norton, 1990, 372–394.

Corbett, Edward P. J. *Classical Rhetoric for the Modern Student*. 2nd ed. New York: Oxford University Press, 1971.

Corder, James W. "Some of What I Learned at a Rhetoric Conference." *Freshman English News*, 15.1 (1986): 11–12.

Covino, William A. *The Art of Wondering: A Revisionist Return to the History of Rhetoric*. Portsmouth, NH: Boynton/Cook–Heinemann, 1988.

———. *Forms of Wondering: A Dialogue on Writing, for Writers*. Portsmouth, NH: Boynton/Cook, 1990.

Crowley, Sharon. *Ancient Rhetorics for Contemporary Students*. New York: MacMillan, 1994.

———. *The Methodical Memory: Invention in Current-Traditional Rhetoric*. Carbondale: Southern Illinois University Press, 1990.

———. "Modern Rhetoric and Memory." In Reynolds, *Rhetorical Memory and Delivery* 31–44.

———. *A Teacher's Guide to Deconstruction*. Urbana: National Council of Teachers of English, 1989.

Culler, Jonathan. "Literary Competence." In Richter 917–929.

Cypert, Rick. "Memory: A Step Toward Invention." Annual Meeting of Conference on College Composition and Communication, Atlanta, GA, March 1987. ERIC document ED280 036.

————. "A Return to the Treasure-House of Invention: Memory in the Composition Classroom." *Freshman English News*, 17.2 (1989): 35–38.

Davidson, Arnold E., and Cathy N. "Decoding the Hemingway Hero in *The Sun Also Rises*." In *New Essays on The Sun Also Rises*. Ed. Linda Wagner-Martin. New York: Cambridge University Press, 1987: 83–107.

Derrida, Jacques. *Memoires: for Paul de Man*. New York: Columbia University Press, 1986.

————. "Plato's Pharmacy." In *Dissemination*. Trans. Barbara Johnson. Chicago: University of Chicago Press, 1972: 63–171.

————. "Structure, Sign, and Play in the Discourse of the Human Sciences." In Richter 959–971.

Descartes, Rene. *The Philosophical Works of Descartes*. Trans. E.S. Haldane and G.T.R. Ross. New York: Dover, 1955.

Eagleton, Mary, ed. *Feminist Literary Theory: A Reader*. Oxford: Basil Blackwell, 1986.

Eagleton, Terry. *Literary Theory: An Introduction*. Minneapolis: University of Minnesota Press, 1983.

Elbow, Peter. *Writing Without Teachers*. New York: Oxford University Press, 1973.

Eliot, T. S. *Four Quartets*. New York: Harcourt Brace and Company, 1943.

Emerson, Ralph Waldo. "The Poet." In Richter 358–369.

Emig, Janet. *The Web of Meaning: Essays on Writing, Teaching, Learning, and Thinking*. Ed. Dixie Goswami and Maureen Butler. Upper Montclair, NJ: Boynton Cook, 1983.

Enos, Richard L. Review of Winifred B. Horner's *Rhetoric in the Classical Tradition*. *Rhetoric Review*, 7.1 (1988): 169–170.

Erdrich, Louise. *Love Medicine*. New York: Holt, 1984.

Faigley, Lester. "Competing Theories of Process: A Critique and a Proposal. *College English* 48.6 (1986): 527–542.

Fetterley, Judith. *The Resisting Reader: A Feminist Approach to American Fiction*. Bloomington: Indiana University Press, 1978.

Finney, Ben. "Myth, Experiment, and the Reinvention of Polynesian Voyaging." *American Anthropologist*, 93.2 (June 1991): 383–404.

Flanagan, Owen. *The Science of the Mind*. 2nd ed. Cambridge: MIT Press, 1991.

Flower, Linda. "Cognition, Context, and Theory Building." *College Composition and Communication* 40.3 (1989): 282–311.

———— and John R. Hayes. "The Cognition of Discovery: Defining a Rhetorical Problem." *College Composition and Communication* 31 (1980): 21–32.

————. "A Cognitive Process Theory of Writing." *College Composition and Communication*, 33(1981): 365–387.

————. "Images, Plans and Prose: The Representation of Meaning in Writing." *Written Communication* 1.1 (1984): 120–160.

Flynn, Elizabeth. "Gender and Reading." *College English* 45.3 (1983): 236–253.

Foucault, Michel. *The Foucault Reader*. Ed. Peter Rabinov Harmondsworth: Penguin, 1986.

Freire, Paulo. *Education for Critical Consciousness*. New York: Continuum, 1989.

Freud, Sigmund. "Creative Writers and Daydreaming." In Richter 651–656.

————. *An Outline of Psychoanalysis*. Trans. James Strachey. New York: Norton, 1949.

Friedan, Betty. *The Feminine Mystique*. New York: W. W. Norton, 1965.

Frye, Northrop. *Anatomy of Criticism*. Princeton: Princeton University Press, 1957.

————. "The Archetypes of Literature." In Richter 677–685.

Fulwiler, Toby, Ed. *The Journal Book*. Portsmouth, NH: Boynton/Cook, 1987.

Garcia Marquez, Gabriel. *Love in the Time of Cholera*. Trans. Edith Grossman. New York: Alfred A. Knopf, 1988.

Gardner, Howard. *Frames of Mind: The Theory of Multiple Intelligences*. New York: Basic Books, 1983.

————. "Mind Explorers Merge Their Maps." *The New York Times* 8 February 1991, C8.

Gates, Henry Louis. *The Signifying Monkey: A Theory of Afro-American Literary Criticism*. New York: Oxford University Press, 1988. Excerpted in Bizzell and Herzberg 1193–1223.

Gilchrist, Ellen. *Light Can Be Both Wave and Particle: A Book of Stories*. Boston: Little, Brown, 1989.

Gilligan, Carol. *In a Different Voice*. Cambridge: Harvard University Press, 1982.

Goethals, George R., and Paul R. Solomon. "Interdisciplinary Perspectives on the Study of Memory." In Solomon, Goethals, Kelly, and Stephens 1–13.

Golden, James A., and Edward P. J. Corbett. *The Rhetoric of Blair, Campbell, and Whately*. New York: Holt, Rinehart and Winston, 1968.

Greene, Gayle. "Feminist Fiction and the Uses of Memory." *Signs: Journal of Women in Culture and Society* 16.2 (1991): 290–321.

Grimshaw, Jean. *Philosophy and Feminist Thinking*. Minneapolis: University of Minnesota Press, 1986.

Gronbeck, Bruce E. "The Spoken and the Seen: The Phonocentric Dimensions of Rhetorical Discourse." In Reynolds, *Rhetorical Memory and Delivery* 139–156.

Gubar, Susan. "'The Blank Page' and the Issues of Creativity." In *The New Feminist Criticism: Essays on Women, Literature, and Theory*. Ed. Elaine Showalter. New York: Pantheon Books, 1985, 292–313.

Haefner, Joel. "Democracy, Pedagogy, and the Personal Essay." *College English* 54.2 (1992): 127–137.

Hairston, Maxine. "The Winds of Change: Thomas Kuhn and the Revolution in the Teaching of Writing." *College Composition and Communication* 33 (1982):76–88.

Halloran, S. Michael. "On the End of Rhetoric, Classical and Modern." *College English*, 36.6 (1975): 621–631.

Hardison, O. B., Jr. *Disappearing Through the Skylight: Culture and Technology in the Twentieth Century*. New York: Penguin Books, 1989.

Harris, Jeannette. "Rethinking Invention." *Freshman English News*, 17.1 (1988): 13–16.

Haswell, Richard. "Dark Shadows: The Fate of Writers at the Bottom." *College Composition and Communication* 39.3 (1988): 303–315.

Havelock, Eric A. *The Muse Learns to Write: Reflections on Orality and Literacy from Antiquity to the Present*. New Haven: Yale University Press, 1986.

Heidegger, Martin. *Being and Time*. Trans. John Macquarrie and E. Robinson. New York: Harper, 1962.

———. *On the Way to Language*. Trans. Peter D. Hertz. New York: Harper and Row, 1971.

———. *What Is Called Thinking?* New York: Harper and Row, 1968.

Hemingway, Ernest. *The Garden of Eden*. New York: MacMillan, 1986.

Hilts, Philip J. "A Brain Unit Seen as Index for Recalling Memories." *New York Times*, 24 Sept. 1991, C1,1+.

Holland, Norman N. *5 Readers Reading*. New Haven: Yale University Press, 1975.

Horner, Winifred B. *Rhetoric in the Classical Tradition*. New York: St. Martin's, 1988.

Hume, David. *An Enquiry Concerning Human Understanding*. Oxford, England: Clarendon Press, 1748.

Hurlbert, C. Mark. "The Signifying Process of the Proper Name: Peirce, Proust, Barthes and Derrida." *Perspective: A Journal of the English Department* (Indiana University of Pennsylvania) 2 (1986): 9–23.

——— and Michael Blitz, eds. *Composition and Resistance*. Portsmouth, NH: Boynton/Cook, 1991.

Husserl, Edmund. *Ideas: General Introduction to Pure Phenomenology*. Trans. W.R. Gibson. London: Allen and Unwin, 1931.

Hutchinson, Robert J. "Nainoa Thompson and the Lost Art of Polynesian Navigation." *Oceans*, August 1988, 18–23+.

Hutton, Patrick H. "The Art of Memory Reconceived: From Rhetoric to Psychoanalysis." *Journal of the History of Ideas* 48(July–Sept. 1987): 371–392.

———. *History as an Art of Memory*. Hanover: University Press of New England, 1993.

Iser, Wolfgang. "The Reading Process: A Phenomenological Approach. In Richter 1219–1232.

Jakobsen, Roman, and Claude Levi-Strauss. "Charles Baudelaire's 'Les Chats.'" In Richter 868–877.

Jameson, Frederic. *Political Unconscious: Narrative as a Socially Symbolic Act*. Ithaca, NY: Cornell University Press, 1981.

Janeczko, Paul B., ed. *Poetspeak: In Their Work, About Their Work*. New York: Bradbury Press, 1983.

Jauss, Hans Robert. "Literary History as a Challenge to Literary Theory." In Richter 1197–1218.

Jay, Gregory S. "The Subject of Pedagogy: Lessons in Psychoanalysis and Politics." *College English* 49.7 (1987): 785–800.

Jenkins, James J. "Language and Memory." In *Communication, Language and Meaning.* Ed. George A. Miller. New York: Basic Books, 1973, 159–171.

Johnson, Barbara, and Marjorie Garber. "Secret Sharing: Reading Conrad Psychoanalytically." *College English* 49.6 (1987): 628–640.

Juncker, Clara. "Writing (with) Cixous." *College English,* 50.4 (1988): 424–436.

Jung, Carl G. *The Archetypes and the Collective Unconscious.* Trans. R. F. C. Hull. Princeton: Princeton University Press, 1959.

————. "On the Relation of Analytical Psychology to Poetry." In Richter 656–666.

————. *Psychological Types or the Psychology of Individuation.* Trans. H.G. Barnes. New York: Harcourt, Brace, 1923.

Kail, Robert V. "The Locus of Word-Finding Problems in Language-Impaired Children." In Solomon, Goethals, Kelly, and Stephens 181–197.

Kelly, George A. *The Psychology of Personal Constructs.* New York: W. W. Norton, 1955.

Kennedy, George A. *Classical Rhetoric and Its Christian and Secular Tradition from Ancient to Modern Times.* Chapel Hill: University of North Carolina Press, 1989.

Kingsolver, Barbara. *Animal Dreams.* New York: Harper Collins Publishers, 1991.

Klatzky, Roberta. *Memory and Awareness: An Information– Processing Perspective.* New York: W. H. Freeman, 1984.

Kolodny, Annette. "Gender and Interpretation of Literary Texts." In *The New Feminist Criticism: Essays on Women, Literature, and Theory.* Ed. Elaine Showalter. New York: Pantheon Books, 1985: 46–62.

Kotulak, Robert. "Scientists Hope to Tap Brain's Fountain of Youth." *Denver Post,* 30 September 1994, A21+.

Krell, David F. *Of Memory, Reminiscence, and Writing: On the Verge.* Bloomington: Indiana University Press, 1990.

Kristeva, Julia. "The Bounded Text." In Richter 989–1005.

————. *Revolution in Poetic Language.* Trans. Margaret Waller. New York: Columbia University Press, 1984.

Kuchler, Susanne, and Walter Melion, eds. *Images of Memory: On Remembering and Representation.* Washington, DC: Smithsonian, 1991.

LeFevre, Karen Burke. *Invention as a Social Act.* Carbondale: Southern Illinois University Press, 1987.

Linden, Eugene. "Lost Tribes, Lost Knowledge." *TIME,* 23 September 1991, 46–56.

Locke, John. *An Essay Concerning Human Understanding.* London: Holt, 1689.

Loftus, Elizabeth F. *Eyewitness Testimony.* Cambridge: Harvard University Press, 1979.

————. *Memory: Surprising New Insights Into How We Remember and Why We Forget.* Reading, MA: Addison-Wesley, 1980.

Lord, A. B. *The Singer of Tales.* Cambridge: Harvard University Press, 1980. Excerpted in Neisser, *Memory Observed: Remembering in Natural Contexts* 243–257.

Lu, Min-zhan. "From Silence to Words: Writing as Struggle." *College English* 49.4 (1987): 437–448.

Luria, Aleksandr R. *The Mind of a Mnemonist.* New York: Basic Books, 1968.

Magee, Bryan. *The Great Philosophers: An Introduction to Western Philosophy.* New York: Oxford University Press, 1987.

Mahony, Patrick. "McLuhan in the Light of Classical Rhetoric." *College Composition and Communication,* 20(Feb. 1969): 12–17.

Marius, Richard D. "On Academic Discourse." *ADE Bulletin* 96 (Fall 1990): 4–7.

Marc, David. "Mass Memory: The Past in the Age of Television." In Reynolds, *Rhetorical Memory and Delivery* 125–138.

Matalene, Carolyn. "Contrastive Rhetoric: An American Writing Teacher in China." *College English* 47.8 (1985): 789–808.

McGaugh, James L. "Modulation of Memory Storage Processes." In Solomon, Goethals, Kelly, and Stephens 33–64.

McLuhan, Marshall. *Understanding Media: The Extensions of Man.* New York: McGraw-Hill, 1964.

Melchert, Norman. *The Great Conversation: A Historical Introduction to Philosophy.* Mountain View, CA: Mayfield, 1991.

Miller, Susan. *Textual Carnivals: The Politics of Composition.* Carbondale: Southern Illinois University Press, 1991.

Moffett, James. *Active Voices IV.* Upper Montclair, NJ: Boynton/Cook, 1986.

Momaday, N. Scott. *The Way to Rainy Mountain.* Albuquerque: University of New Mexico Press, 1976.

Montale, Eugenio. "The Second Life of Art." In *The Second Life of Art: Selected Essays of Eugenio Montale,* Ed. and Trans. Jonathan Galassi. New York: Ecco Press, 1982, 20–24.

Morris, Peter E., and Martin A. Conway. *The Psychology of Memory.* 3 vols. New York: New York University Press, 1993.

Morrison, Toni. *Beloved.* New York: Penguin Books, 1988.

Murray, Donald M. *Expecting the Unexpected: Teaching Myself—and Others—to Read and Write.* Portsmouth, NH: Boynton/Cook, 1989.

————. *Shoptalk: Learning to Write with Writers.* Portsmouth, NH: Boynton/Cook, 1990.

————. "Writing and Teaching for Surprise." *College English,* 46.1 (1984): 1–7.

Nabokov, Vladimir. *Speak Memory: An Autobiography Revisited.* Rev. ed. New York: G. P. Putnam's Sons, 1966.

Neel, Jasper P. *Plato, Derrida, and Writing.* Carbondale: Southern Illinois University Press, 1988.

Neisser, Ulric. "Domains of Memory." In Solomon, Goethals, Kelly, and Stephens 67–83.

————. *Memory Observed: Remembering in Natural Contexts.* New York: W. H. Freeman, 1982.

Nelson, Katherine. "Remembering: A Functional Developmental Perspective." In Solomon, Goethals, Kelly, and Stephens 127–150.

Nickerson, Raymond S., and Marilyn Jager Adams. "Long Term Memory for a Common Object." In Neisser, *Memory,* 163–175.

Nietzsche, Friedrich. "On Truth and Lies in a Nonmoral Sense." Trans. Daniel Breazeale. In Bizzell and Herzberg 888–896.

————. *The Philosophy of Nietzsche.* New York: Mentor Books, 1965.

————. *The Use and Abuse of History.* Trans. Adrian Collins. New York: The Liberal Arts Press, 1949.

North, Stephen M. *The Making of Knowledge in Composition:* Portsmouth, NH: Boynton/Cook, 1987.

Olsen, Tillie. "One Out of Twelve: Women Who Are Writers in Our Century." In Ruddick and Daniels 323–340.

Olson, Gary A. "Social Construction and Composition Theory: A Conversation with Richard Rorty. *Journal of Advanced Composition,* 9 (1989): 1–9.

Olster, Stacy. *Reminiscence and Re-Creation in Contemporary American Fiction.* New York: Cambridge University Press, 1989.

Ong, Walter J. *Orality and Literacy: The Technologizing of the Word.* New York: Methuen, 1982.

————. *Ramus, Method, and the Decay of Dialogue.* Cambridge: Harvard University Press, 1958.

————. *Rhetoric, Romance and Technology: Studies in the Interaction of Expression and Culture.* Ithaca: Cornell University Press, 1971.

Ostrom, Thomas M. "Three Catechisms of Social Memory." In Solomon, Goethals, Kelly, and Stephens 198–220.

Palmer, Donald. *Does the Center Hold? An Introduction to Western Philosophy.* Mountain View, CA: Mayfield, 1991.

————. *Looking at Philosophy: The Unbearable Heaviness of Philosophy Made Lighter.* Mountain View, CA: Mayfield, 1988.

Perl, Sondra. "Understanding Composing." In *The Writing Teacher's Sourcebook.* Ed. Gary Tate and Edward P. J. Corbett. New York: Oxford University Press, 1988, 113–118. Reprinted from *College Composition and Communication,* 31 (Dec. 1980): 363–369.

Philipson, Morris. *Outline of a Jungian Aesthetics.* Evanston: Northwestern University Press, 1963.

Piercy, Marge. "Unlearning to Not Speak." In *Responding to Literature*. Ed. Judith A. Stanford. Mountain View, CA: Mayfield, 1992. 1179–1180.

Pigott, Margaret B. "Sexist Roadblocks in Inventing, Focusing, and Writing." *College English* 40 (1979): 922–927.

Pirsig, Robert. *Zen and the Art of Motorcycle Maintenance*. New York: Bantam, 1976.

Plato. *Phaedrus*. Trans. H. N. Fowler. In *The Rhetorical Tradition*. Ed. Patricia Bizzell and Bruce Herzberg. Boston: Bedford Books, 1990. 113–143.

————. *Theaetatus*. Trans. Frances M. Cornford. NY: Bobbs-Merrill, 1934.

Postman, Neil. *Amusing Ourselves to Death: Public Discourse in the Age of Show Business*. New York, Penguin Books, 1985.

Proust, Marcel. *Remembrance of Things Past*. New York: Random House, 1934.

Provenzo, Eugene F., Jr. *Video Kids: Making Sense of Nintendo*. Cambridge: Harvard University Press, 1991.

Quintilian. *The Institutio Oratorio*. Trans. H. E. Butler. Cambridge: Harvard University Press, 1970.

Ramus, Peter. *Arguments in Rhetoric Against Quintilian*. 1549; Trans. Carole Newlands. Dekalb: Northern Illinois University Press, 1986.

Reed, W. Michael, and Thomas M. Sherman. "Using Memory During Prewriting: The Comparative Effects of External Storage and Idea Organization on the Syntactic Complexity and Quality of Basic and Honor Writers' Narrative Essays." *Research and Teaching in Developmental Education*, 7.2 (1991): 67–79.

Reynolds, John Frederick. "Concepts of Memory in Contemporary Composition." *Rhetoric Society Quarterly*, XIX.3 (1989): 245–252.

————. "Memory Issues in Composition Studies." In Reynolds, *Rhetorical Memory and Delivery* 1–15.

————."Redefining 'The Classical Tradition' in a New Writing Textbook. Review of *Rhetoric in the Classical Tradition* by Winifred Bryan Horner. *Rhetoric Society Quarterly*, 18.2 (1988): 201–203.

————, ed. *Rhetorical Memory and Delivery: Classical Concepts for Contemporary Composition and Communication*. Hillsdale: Lawrence Erlbaum Associates, 1993.

Rhetorica Ad Herennium. Trans. Harry Caplan. Cambridge: Harvard University Press, 1954.

Rich, Adrienne. "Diving Into the Wreck." In *The Norton Anthology of Literature by Women: The Tradition in English*. Ed. Sandra M. Gilbert and Susan Gubar. New York: W. W. Norton, 1985. 2032–2035.

————. Foreword. In Ruddick and Daniels xiii–xxiv.

————. "When We the Dead Awaken: Writing as Re–Vision." In *The Norton Anthology of Literature About Women: The Tradition in English*. Ed. Sandra M. Gilbert and Susan Gubar. New York: W. W. Norton, 1985. 2044–2056.

Richter, David H., ed. *The Critical Tradition: Classic Texts and Contemporary Trends*. New York: St. Martin's, 1989.

Robbe-Grillet, Alain. *In the Labyrinth*. In *Two Novels by Robbe-Grillet*. Trans. Richard Howard. New York: Grove Press, 1965.

Robinson, Jay L. "Literacy in the Department of English." *Conversation on the Written Word: Essays on Language and Literacy*. Portsmouth, NH: Boynton/Cook, 1990.

Rohman, D. Gordon. "Prewriting: The Stage of Discovery in the Writing Process." *CCC* 16 (1965): 106–112.

Rorty, Richard. *Philosophy and the Mirror of Nature*. Princeton: Princeton University Press, 1979.

————. "Epistemological Behaviorism and the De-transcendentalization of Analytic Philosophy." In *Hermeneutics and Praxis*, Ed. Robert Hollinger. Notre Dame: University of Notre Dame Press, 1985, 89–121.

————. *Contingency, Irony and Solidarity*. New York: Cambridge University Press, 1989.

Rosenblatt, Louise. *Literature as Exploration*. New York: Appleton-Century, 1938.

Rubin, David C. *Autobiographical Memory*. New York: Cambridge University Press, 1986.

Ruddick, Sara, and Pamela Daniels, eds. *Working It Out: 23 Women Writers, Artists, Scientists and Scholars Talk About Their Lives and Work.* New York: Pantheon Books, 1977.

Salaman, Esther. "A Collection of Moments." In *A Collection of Moments: A Study of Involuntary Memory.* London: Longman, 1970. Rpt. in Neisser, *Memory Observed: Remembering in Natural Contexts* 49–63.

Schachtel, Ernest G. "On Memory and Childhood Amnesia." *Psychiatry* 10 (1947): 1–26.

Selden, Raman. *A Reader's Guide to Contemporary Literary Theory.* 2nd ed. Lexington: University of Kentucky Press, 1987.

Shelnutt, Eve. *Writing: A Translation of Memory.* New York: MacMillan, 1990.

Silko, Leslie Marmon. *Ceremony.* New York: Viking Penguin, 1988.

Simonson, Rick, and Scott Walker. *The Graywolf Annual Five: Multicultural Literacy.* St. Paul: Graywolf Press, 1988.

Smith, Frank. *Joining the Literacy Club.* Portsmouth, NH: Heinemann-Boynton/Cook, 1988.

———. *Understanding Reading.* Hillsdale, NJ: Lawrence Erlbaum Associates, 1988.

Solomon, Paul R, George R. Goethals, Colleen M. Kelley, and Benjamin R. Stephens, eds. *Memory: Interdisciplinary Approaches.* New York: Springer-Verlag, 1989.

Sosnoski, James J. "Students as Theorists: Collaborative Hypertexts." In *Practicing Theory in Introductory College Literature Courses.* Ed. James M. Calahan and David B. Downing. Urbana, IL: National Council of Teachers of English, 1991. 271–290.

Spender, Dale. *Man Made Language.* Boston: Routledge and Kegan Paul, 1980.

Squire, Larry S. "Mechanisms of Memory." *Science,* 232 (June 1986): 1612–1619.

Stark, John O. *The Literature of Exhaustion: Borges, Nabokov, and Barth.* Durham, NC: Duke University Press, 1974.

Stern, J. P. "Nietzsche and the Idea of Metaphor." In *Nietzsche: Imagery and Thought.* Ed. Malcolm Pasley. Berkeley: University of California Press, 1978.

Stevick, Philip. "Literature." In *The Postmodern Moment: A Handbook of Contemporary Innovation in the Arts.* Ed. Stanley Trachtenberg. Westport, CT: Greenwood Press, 1985, 135–156.

Stratton, George M. "The Mnemonic Feat of the 'Shass Pollak.'" *Psychological Review,* 24 (1917): 244–247. In Neisser, *Memory Observed: Remembering in Natural Contexts* 311–314.

Strickland, Kathleen and James. *Uncovering the Curriculum: Whole Language in Secondary and Post-Secondary Classrooms.* Portsmouth, NH: Boynton/Cook, 1993.

Tannen, Deborah. *You Just Don't Understand: Men and Women in Conversation.* New York: William Morrow, 1990.

Thompson, Richard F. "A Model System Approach to Memory." In Solomon, Goethals, Kelly, and Stephens 17–32.

Tierney, Robert J., and F. David Pearson. "Toward a Composing Model of Reading." In *Perspectives in Literacy.* Ed. Eugene R. Kintgen, Barry M. Kroll, and Mike Rose. Carbondale: Southern Illinois University Press, 1988.

Velie, Alan R. *Four American Indian Literary Masterpieces.* Norman: University of Oklahoma Press, 1982.

Ventura, Michael. "Report from El Dorado." In Simonson and Walker 173–188.

Vico, Giambattista. *The New Science of Giambattista Vico.* 1725. Trans. Thomas G. Bergen and Max H. Fisch. New York: Cornell University Press, 1984.

———. *On the Study Methods of Our Times.* Trans. Elio Gianturco. Excerpted in Bizzell and Herzberg 715–727.

Wallace, Doris B., and Howard E. Gruber. *Creative People at Work: Twelve Cognitive Case Studies.* New York: Oxford University Press, 1989.

Welch, Kathleen E. "Autobiography and Advanced College Writing." 38th Annual Meeting of the Conference on College Composition and Communication. Atlanta, March 1987. ERIC ED 281 229.

———. *The Contemporary Reception of Classical Rhetoric: Appropriations of Classical Rhetoric.* Hillsdale, NJ: Lawrence Erlbaum Associates, Inc., 1990.

————. "Electrifying Classical Rhetoric: Ancient Media, Modern Technology, and Contemporary Composition." *Journal of Advanced Composition* 10.1 (1990): 22–38.

————. "The Platonic Paradox: Plato's Rhetoric in Contemporary Rhetoric and Composition Studies." *Written Communication*, 5.1 (1988): 3–21.

White, Hayden. *Metahistory: The Historical Imagination in the Nineteenth Century*. Baltimore: Johns Hopkins University Press, 1974.

Witte, Stephen P. "Pre-text and Composing." *College Composition and Communication*, 38.4 (1987): 397–425.

Wordsworth, William. Preface to *Lyrical Ballads*. 1802. In Richter 285–298.

Wyer, Robert S., Jr. "Social Memory and Social Judgment." In Solomon, Goethals, Kelly, and Stephens 243–270.

Yates, Frances A. *The Art of Memory*. Chicago: University of Chicago Press, 1966.

————. *Giordano Bruno and the Hermetic Tradition*. London: Routledge and Kegan Paul Ltd., 1964.

Young, Richard E. "Paradigms and Problems: Needed Research in Rhetorical Invention." In *Research in Composing*. Ed. Charles Cooper and Lee Odell. Urbana: NCTE, 1978: 29–47.

———— and Patricia Sullivan. "Why Write?" In *Essays in Classical Rhetoric and Modern Discourse*. Ed. Robert J. Connors, Lisa S. Ede, and Andrea A. Lunsford. Carbondale: Southern Illinois University Press, 1984: 215–225.

Zawacki, Terry Myers. "Recomposing as a Woman—An Essay in Different Voices." *College Composition and Communication* 43.1 (1992): 32–38.

Zola-Morgan, Stuart, and Larry R. Squire. "The Primate Hippocampal Formation: Evidence for a Time-Limited Role in Memory Storage." *Science,* 12 October 1990, 288–290.

Author Index

Subject Index

T

Taboos, of writing and culture, 123
Teaching of memory, 105–108
Theuth, 13
Time, 70, 71, 72, 74, 82
    necessity of for writing, 105
Tip-of-Tongue (TOT) phenomenon, 45
Treasure-house, *see* Storehouse
Trinity of the soul, memory as part of the, 15

U

Unconscious, 35, 78, 80, 84, 85, 90, 99
Universal memory, 77, *see also* Cultural memory, Racial memory
University, rhetoric of the, *see* Rhetoric, academic
Unreliability of memory, 35, 36, 44

Unthought (Heidegger), 63

V

Vico, Giambattista, 23–24, 26, 93
Voice, as metaphor for development, 122

W

Waxen tablet, image of memory as, 10, 11, 12, 24, 67, 82
Whateley, Richard, 25, 26
Wittgenstein, Ludwig, 64, 65
Women's Ways of Knowing, 88, 105
Wonder, writing as, 93, 98, 103
Writing, as act of memory, 2, 6, 10, 12–13, 16, 22, 27, 30, 39, 43, 71, 73, 76, 79, 80, 82, 85–86, 91–108, 114, 127
Writing process, *see* Composing process